CHEROKEE FREEDMEN

The Cooper Family in Fort Gibson, Indian Territory, in the late 1800's
    donated by Jessie Mae (Cooper) Coulter.

CHEROKEE FREEDMEN:
We Are Cherokee

Part of
The Black Cherokee Series

Ty "GWY" Wilson
A Cherokee historian from the Cherokee Nation of Oklahoma

[BLK-FTHR Media/PE Church]
CHEROKEE NATION, USA

DEDICATION

This book is for Jessie Mae Coulter, who was born, raised, married, had children, and lived her entire life in the Cherokee Nation. Jessie Mae was always told she didn't look Black, so the world doubted her Blackness. Yet on the Dawes Rolls for her family, some of whom appear in the picture on the cover, were labeled as Freedmen. So, the government doubted Jessie's Nativeness. She inspired me by sharing her family pictures and her life story. Granny, this book is for your memories.

This book is for the Cherokee elders in all the Cherokee communities, who never treated Black Cherokees any differently than any other Cherokee.

For all the Black Cherokees.

For the ones who were reduced to "et al." in court records.

And for the families who never stopped belonging anyway.

For the Lee Street neighborhood in Tahlequah and every road that leads back home.

Table of Contents

EPIGRAPH

My family tree had a lot of branches.
　　　　Some of us had blood quantum cards.
Some of us didn't.

But my Black Cherokee elders always said,
 "We are all Cherokee."

Series Introduction

The Black Cherokee Series

By Ty "GWY" Wilson, a Cherokee historian from the Cherokee Nation of Oklahoma.

This book is part of a larger body of work. A multi-volume series dedicated to telling the full, unbroken story of Black Cherokees. That story includes the Black people who married into Cherokee families and their descendants; the free Black people who lived in and participated fully in Cherokee society when the Cherokee Nation was a separate entity from the United States; and the Cherokee Freedmen and their descendants who were promised citizenship under the Treaty of 1866. Together, they form one unbroken story of Black Cherokees. A story that has always existed, even when the record tried to hide it.

For generations, Black Cherokee stories have been pushed to the margins, reduced to footnotes, or treated as controversies instead of lived realities. But our history is not an "issue." It is not a debate. It is not an afterthought. It is a central strand in the story of the Cherokee people.

This series exists to bring that truth forward.

Each book in this collection focuses on a different part of Black Cherokee history from the earliest presence of African and Indigenous people in the Southeast, to the Trail of Tears, to the Civil War in Indian Territory, to the Treaty of 1866, to the Dawes Rolls and allotment, to Oklahoma statehood and Jim Crow, to the modern legal battles that forced the Nation and the United States to confront the promises written in law.

Together, these books form a single narrative:
a story of survival, belonging, erasure, resistance, and truth.

I write this series not as an outsider or an academic observer, but as Ty "GWY" Wilson. A Black Cherokee from Tahlequah, raised in the neighborhoods, churches, powwows, ball courts, and communities that shaped Cherokee life long before paperwork tried to divide us. My identity was lived before it was ever questioned. My understanding of Cherokee belonging comes from elders, family, neighbors, and the everyday rhythms of Native life in Northeastern Oklahoma.

This series is for the people whose names were turned into "et al" in documents.

For the families who carried Cherokee identity through silence and suspicion.

For the elders who told the truth even when the record did not.

For the descendants who refused to disappear.

For the Nation that is stronger when it honors all its people.

These books are not written to reopen wounds.

They are written to close them with truth, with integrity, and with the full story restored.

This is Black Cherokee history.
This is Cherokee history.
This is our whole story.

Author's Note

I wrote this book as a Black Cherokee from Tahlequah, not as an outsider studying Cherokee history. But as someone raised inside it. My earliest memories are Cherokee memories: church pews filled with familiar faces, basketball tournaments in all-Indian leagues, powwows where the drumbeat felt like home, and elders who never once questioned whether I belonged. They didn't use words like "Freedmen" or "by blood." They just said we were Cherokee.

This book grew out of that lived truth.

I didn't write it to win an argument. I wrote it because I've watched too many people I love, neighbors, cousins, elders, veterans, church leaders, get reduced to paperwork and "et al." in court cases. I wrote it because I've seen how colonial categories can be used to divide a Nation that survived removal, war, allotment, and statehood. I wrote it because the story of Black Cherokees is not a footnote. It is part of the spine.

I wrote it because the people who carried out this fight were not abstractions to me.

Bernice Riggs was an elder in my neighborhood and my Black Cherokee church.

Reverend Robert Nero was someone I fellowshipped with at my church, his church, and other Black Cherokee churches across the Nation.

Charlene White is my cousin, and she was my next-door neighbor growing up.

Ralph Threat is a U.S. veteran and a family friend, connected through some of my people, even though we aren't directly kin.

These are not case names. They are my people.

And I moved through Native spaces, traditional communities, churches, powwows, sports tournaments, the way people move when they belong. I dated and married Native women, raised Native children, and started businesses in Cherokee communities. Not because I was claiming something. But because it was already mine.

This book is my contribution to a truth that has always been bigger than paperwork: that Cherokee identity is lived, not assigned; that treaties matter; that kinship matters; that history matters; and that Black Cherokee families have been part of this Nation's story since way before the Trail of Tears.

If this book does anything, I hope it helps us remember that telling the whole truth does not weaken the Cherokee Nation. It strengthens it.

Because a Cherokee Nation that knows its full story and honors all its people is not a Nation that can be divided by paper.

And that is the Cherokee future I believe in.

PREFACE

I was born and raised in Tahlequah, Oklahoma, the capital of the Cherokee Nation. For most people, that fact alone tells them who they think I am. For others, it raises questions they believe I should have to answer.

This book exists because I am tired of those questions being asked in bad faith.

I am a Cherokee citizen. I am also a historian, an artist, a community leader, and an entrepreneur. More importantly, I am someone who grew up submerged in Cherokee stories spoken and unspoken. I also learned that some histories were celebrated while others were carefully avoided. I learned which ancestors were honored publicly. And which were only mentioned in whispers, if they were mentioned at all.

The history of Black Cherokees, which includes Cherokee Freedmen, lives in those silences.

This book is not written to provoke guilt, nor to demand sympathy. It is written to tell the truth — the kind of truth that survives in courtrooms, archives, family stories, and lived experiences. The kind of truth that refuses to be simplified into slogans or reduced to paperwork.

Before there were rolls, before there was blood quantum, before there were federal categories that divided us into neat boxes, Cherokee identity was built on kinship, responsibility, and belonging. Citizenship was not a line on a ledger. It was participation in the life of the Nation. That reality matters because much of the modern debate around Cherokee Freedmen begins from a false premise: that identity has always been racial, fixed, and bureaucratic. It has not.

Slavery, too, did not arrive in Indian Country in a vacuum. Native people were enslaved by European colonists long before some Native nations, including the Cherokee, adopted systems of African chattel slavery under pressure, coercion, and economic manipulation. None of this history is clean. None of it should be. But avoiding it has caused more harm than facing it ever could.

The term "Freedmen" is often used today as if it were a cultural identity or a separate people. It is not. It is a legal designation imposed by the United States after the Civil War, one that came with promises, written promises, of citizenship, land, and equality within the Cherokee Nation. Those promises were not optional. They were treaty obligations. And treaties are the backbone of Native sovereignty, whether they are convenient or not.

Cherokee Freedmen are not outsiders knocking on the door of the Nation. They are the descendants of people who lived, labored, fought, worshiped, married, and raised families within Cherokee society, often under conditions they did not choose. Their history is inseparable from Cherokee history, not because anyone wishes it to be, but because it already is.

I wrote this book for those who were told they did not belong, despite knowing in their bones that they did. I wrote it for Cherokee citizens who want a fuller, more honest understanding of our past. I wrote it for students, educators, and community members who are tired of narratives that flatten complex histories into accusations or denials.

Most of all, I wrote it because sovereignty without truth is fragile, and identity without integrity cannot last.

We are still here.

And we are Cherokee.

Acknowledgements

This series of books could not have come into being without the love, labor, and prayers of many people, and it is my honor to thank them here.

First, I give thanks to the Great Spirit and to my Cherokee and Black ancestors, whose strength, survival, and stories are the true foundation of every page. I am especially grateful for the elders who share their memories. Who corrected my misunderstandings and reminded me that our history lives not only in documents, but in kitchens, church pews, car rides, and front porches.

To Jessie May Coulter, for donating the picture of her ancestors that appears on the cover of this book, and for being one of the original members of the CBIHP Foundation. Thank you for always pushing me to keep going. Your presence is missing.

To the people of the Lee Street neighborhood in Tahlequah, Oklahoma. The community that raised me and showed me what it means to belong. I owe a debt I can never fully repay. The sounds of Sunday morning, the laughter in the park, the quiet wisdom of those who came before us: all those lives between these lines. This book is, in many ways, a love letter to you.

I want to thank the many Native American nations and community organizations who opened their doors and their archives, and who welcomed me into conversations about memory, identity, and truth. To the tribal citizens, cultural keepers, and community historians across the United States who shared stories, photographs, and family records. Thank you for trusting me with your history. Your courage to speak and to remember helped shape the heart of this work.

My deep gratitude goes out to the nonprofits, cultural centers, universities, libraries, and museums that partnered with me, hosted programs, invited me to speak, and supported the ongoing work of preserving and sharing Native and Black Cherokee history. Your staff and volunteers do the quiet, everyday labor that makes books like this possible.

To my colleagues in writing and research, including those with whom I have worked on the Black Cherokee Series and 1st American book series, and Oklahoma Black Cherokees. Thank you for your insight, your scholarship, and your patience. Our discussions, debates, and late-night calls sharpened this project and kept it honest.

I extend special thanks to my mentors, whose guidance and example have meant more than words can say:

Karen "Coody" Cooper, Cherokee historian, for her deep knowledge and steadfast encouragement.

Dr. Daniel Littlefield of the Sequoyah Research Center, for his scholarship and support.

ShIron and Oscar Ray of Legacy-Keepers-R-Us and the Bare Bones Film Festival, for championing independent voices and stories.

Jason Irby of the Jason Irby Innovation Foundation, for his belief in creative vision and community work.

And Selby Minner of the Oklahoma Blues Hall of Fame, for keeping the music—and the stories behind it—alive.

Your mentorship has helped guide my steps through both history and art.

Thank you to Detreck Ridgeway and everyone who participated in making the documentary, The 1st Annual Cherokee History Symposium. As a filmmaker, musician, and visual artist, I am blessed to be part of creative communities that continually inspire me. To my fellow filmmakers, producers, musicians, poets, and designers: thank you for encouraging me to keep telling our stories in every medium available. Your belief in the power of art fuels my own.

I am honored to serve on the boards of the Oklahoma Blues Hall of Fame, the Bare Bones Film Festival, and the Cherokee Nation Freedmen History Advisory Committee. To my fellow board members, staff, and volunteers: thank you for your dedication to preserving history, music, and film, and for reminding me, time and again, that our stories don't just live in books; they live in sound and image, on stages and screens, wherever our people gather.

To my CBIHP Foundation co-founders, Deloris Wilson and Troy Wilson, and to Jessie Mae Coulter and every board member and volunteer who helped with research, outreach, events, and community work behind the scenes: this book carries your fingerprints. Thank you for the countless hours, the road trips, the phone calls, and the unwavering belief that our history is worth fighting for.

To my family and friends, who have stood by me through long research trips, late-night writing sessions, and the emotional weight that comes with digging into painful chapters of our past: your love and understanding gave me the strength to keep going. Thank you for giving me space to do this work and for reminding me to rest when I forgot how.

To my grandparents, Bud Cooper and Minerva Wilson: Thank you for raising me to believe I could do anything with hard work. Your example taught me to be proud of who I am and where I come from.

Finally, to every reader who picks up this book with an open heart: thank you. By choosing to engage with these stories, you become part of the work of preservation. May these pages honor those who came before us and inspire those who are yet to come.

Summary

This book tells the story that has too often been pushed to the margins of Cherokee history: the story of Black Cherokees, Cherokee Freedmen, and the descendants who have lived, loved, built, worshiped, and survived inside the Cherokee Nation for generations.

It traces the full arc of that history from the colonial slave trade and the Trail of Tears, through the Civil War and the Treaty of 1866, through the Dawes Rolls and allotment, through Oklahoma statehood and Jim Crow, and into the modern legal battles that forced the Nation and the United States to confront the promises written in Article 9.

Across these chapters, one truth becomes clear:

Cherokee identity was never meant to be defined by federal paperwork.

It lives through kinship, community, responsibility, and shared survival.

This book shows how colonial systems rolls, blood quantum, racial categories, and disenrollment attempted to divide a people who had already built a shared life. It exposes how the Dawes Rolls froze errors into law, how Jim Crow hardened racial boundaries, and how modern politics revived old divisions under a new language.

But it also documents the courage of those who refused to disappear:

the elders, neighbors, veterans, church leaders, and families who carried the truth forward even when the record tried to erase them. Their names, often reduced to "et al.," are restored here as part of the Nation's living memory.

The book follows the long legal struggle for recognition, culminating in the 2017 federal decision affirming that Freedmen descendants are citizens with "all the rights of native Cherokees," as promised in the Treaty of 1866. It highlights the leadership that chose truth, the institutions that began telling the full story, and the communities that never stopped living it.

At its core, this book is a declaration:

We are Cherokee.

Not because of a roll.

Not because of a fraction.

But because our families lived Cherokee history before removal, through removal, after removal, and into the present.

This is not a story of outsiders seeking entry.

It is a story of citizens reclaiming the truth that was always theirs.

And it is a call for a Cherokee future rooted not in fear, but in integrity, a future where the Nation honors its treaties, its history, and all its people.

Introduction - We Are Cherokee

The question is rarely asked with curiosity.

It is usually asked with an edge, sometimes polite, sometimes openly hostile. But almost always carrying the same assumption: that Cherokee identity can be measured, proven, or denied through a single document, a racial category, or a line on a government roll. For Cherokee Freedmen and their descendants, that assumption has shaped more than a century of exclusion, confusion, and conflict.

This book begins by rejecting that premise.

Cherokee identity did not originate with the United States government. It did not begin with the Dawes Rolls, blood quantum, or post–Civil War classifications. Long before federal agents arrived with clipboards and categories, the Cherokee people governed themselves through kinship systems, clans, shared responsibility, and lived participation in the Nation. Belonging was something practiced, not possessed.

Yet much of the modern debate surrounding Cherokee Freedmen is rooted in a misunderstanding or a deliberate misrepresentation of history. The story is often told as if Freedmen appeared suddenly after emancipation, unconnected to Cherokee life except through slavery, and therefore external to the Nation itself. That version of history is incomplete at best and dishonest at worst.

Cherokee Freedmen did not emerge from nowhere. They are the descendants of Africans and African Americans who lived among the Cherokee before, during, and after removal; of people who labored in Cherokee households and fields; of families who worshiped in Cherokee churches, spoke the language, intermarried, fought in wars, and helped rebuild the Nation after devastation. Some were enslaved. Some were free. Many were both over the course of their lives. All were shaped by Cherokee society and contributed to it.

To understand this history honestly, we must first confront a deeper truth: slavery in what became the United States did not begin with African bodies alone. Native Americans were among the earliest enslaved peoples under European colonization. Entire communities were raided, sold, and forced into labor, often far from their homelands. This system destabilized Indigenous societies, normalized human commodification, and laid the groundwork for racial hierarchies that would later be imposed on both Native and African peoples.

When slavery later took hold within some Native nations, including the Cherokee, it did so in a world already transformed by colonial violence, economic coercion, and U.S. expansion. Acknowledging that context does not erase responsibility, but it does restore complexity, and complexity is essential if we are serious about truth.

The term "Freedman" is a product of that colonial framework. In U.S. law, it described formerly enslaved people after the Civil War. When applied to Native nations, it became a legal classification used by the federal government to organize, control, and ultimately divide tribal citizens. Over time, that label was stripped of its legal meaning and weaponized as a racial boundary. One never intended by Cherokee tradition but enforced through U.S. policy.

This book traces that transformation: from kinship-based belonging to paper-based exclusion; from treaty-guaranteed citizenship to bureaucratic erasure; from shared survival to contested identity. It follows the history of enslaved Africans, free Blacks, Freedmen, and Black Cherokees from the earliest days of contact through removal, emancipation, allotment, statehood, and into the present-day Cherokee Nation.

It is not a legal brief, though it engages in law. It is not an apology, nor an accusation. It is a historical reckoning grounded in evidence, lived experience, and the understanding that nations — like people — must confront their past honestly if they intend to move forward with integrity.

The struggle over Cherokee Freedmen citizenship is often framed as a threat: to sovereignty, to culture, to identity itself. But sovereignty built on selective memory is brittle. Culture guarded by exclusion forgets its own foundations. Identity, when reduced to race and paperwork, loses the very values it claims to protect.

This book asks a different question.

What would it mean for the Cherokee Nation to claim its history, all of it fully, and still say, without hesitation or qualification?

We are Cherokee.

Chapter 1 - Cherokee Identity Before the USA

Before there were rolls, before there were enrollment cards, before a federal agent ever decided to sort Cherokee people into categories, Cherokee identity already existed. It was lived. It was practiced. It was recognized by the community long before anyone outside the Cherokee Nation wrote it down.

That distinction matters.

Much of the modern debate over Cherokee citizenship begins with paperwork, as if documents created the people. They did not. The people came first. The Nation came first. And the standards for belonging came first — rooted not in race, not in fractions, and not in federal definitions, but in relationships.

Belonging Was Not a Document

When Cherokee society developed its systems of identity and governance, it did so for people who lived among one another, who shared responsibility, and who carried history through memory, language, and practice. Identity was not something proven to a distant authority. It was something affirmed daily through participation in the life of the Nation.

A person belonged because they were claimed by family, recognized by community, and accountable to others. That recognition was mutual. You could not simply declare yourself Cherokee. You were Cherokee because Cherokee people knew you as such.

This understanding stands in direct contrast to the American obsession with records, birth certificates, census forms, property deeds, and rolls. Those systems assume identity is something fixed on paper. Cherokee society understood identity as something lived.

Clan and Kinship: The Foundation of Citizenship

Clan was the foundation of Cherokee identity. It determined family relationships, marriage rules, responsibilities, and collective accountability. Cherokee society was matrilineal. Children belonged to their mother's clan, not their father's lineage in the European sense.

This matrilineal structure placed women at the center of identity, continuity, and belonging. Clan membership was not symbolic; it governed daily life. It determined who cared for you, who defended you, and who answered for you if harm occurred.

In this system, identity was relational. It was impossible to separate a person from their people.

What "Fullblood" Meant in Cherokee Society

In traditional Cherokee society, the term now translated as "Fullblood" did not refer to a mathematical measure of ancestry. It did not describe fractions of blood. It had nothing to do with what the United States would later invent as "blood quantum."

A "Fullblood" Cherokee was understood as someone who lived fully within the Cherokee ways.

This meant speaking the language, practicing Cherokee customs, participating in ceremonial life, following clan responsibilities, and living according to Cherokee values. It described cultural immersion and lived practice, not racial purity.

A person could be considered "Fullblood" because they lived traditionally, while another might be considered "mixed" or "assimilated" because they adopted European customs, language, dress, or religion. These distinctions were about the way of life, not genetics.

The U.S. government later stripped this concept of its meaning and replaced it with a racialized system of blood fractions. In doing so, it distorted a Cherokee cultural term into a bureaucratic tool used to divide families. And determine who would count and who would not under federal law.

Adoption and Incorporation: A Living Nation

Cherokee identity was never static. The Nation had long-standing practices of adoption and incorporation. Captives taken during war could be adopted into families. Outsiders could become part of the Nation through marriage, alliance, and community recognition.

These practices were no exception. They were part of how Cherokee society maintained balance and continuity, especially in the face of loss from disease, warfare, and displacement.

Belonging requires responsibility. Those incorporated into the Nation were expected to live by Cherokee norms, honor clan obligations, and contribute to the collective life of the people.

This reality directly challenges modern assumptions that Indigenous nations were historically closed or racially defined. Cherokee belonging was structured, intentional, and relational — not exclusionary by default.

The Arrival of Race and Hierarchy

Race, as enforced by European and American systems, introduced a hierarchy foreign to Cherokee society. It was designed to justify slavery, dispossession, and domination. Over time, these ideas seeped into Indigenous communities under intense pressure.

Missionaries, traders, and federal agents encouraged Cherokee leaders to adopt European social models, including private land ownership, plantation agriculture, and racialized slavery. These changes did not reflect traditional Cherokee values, but they reshaped the Nation's political and economic landscape.

As some Cherokees became more economically aligned with Southern society, distinctions began to form between those who lived traditionally, often described as "Fullblood," and those who embraced European customs. Again, this divide was cultural, not racial.

Why This Matters for Cherokee Freedmen

Understanding Cherokee identity before U.S. interference is essential to understanding the history of Cherokee Freedmen.

If you begin with blood quantum, you accept federal fiction as a Cherokee tradition.
If you begin with rolls, you mistake colonial recordkeeping for Indigenous law.
But if you begin with kinship, clan, cultural practice, and lived responsibility, a different picture emerges.
Cherokee citizenship was never meant to be a racial boundary. It was a bond of relationships and obligation. And when the United States later imposed rigid racial categories onto Cherokee society, it fractured systems that had long allowed for incorporation, complexity, and shared life.

That fracture would have lasting consequences — especially for Black Cherokees, Freedmen, and their descendants, whose belonging had once been understood through participation and kinship but would later be questioned through paperwork and race.

In the next chapter, we will examine how African presence entered Cherokee society, how people of African descent lived among the Cherokee before and after slavery, and how traditional notions of belonging were challenged by a colonial world increasingly obsessed with classification.

Because before the United States decided who counted, the Cherokee Nation already knew how to recognize its own.

CHEROKEE FREEDMEN

Chapter 2 - Kinship, Not Color

If you start Cherokee history from a U.S. perspective, you end up believing race has always been the organizing principle. You end up believing the categories on a federal roll are ancient truths. But the Cherokee Nation did not begin as a paperwork system. And it did not begin as a racial caste system.

It began as a people.

That's why the presence of African people in Cherokee life cannot be treated as a late "addition" or a modern complication. Black presence in Cherokee history is not new. It is not an accident. And it is not limited to slavery. Africans and African Americans were present in Cherokee territory early, and their lives in Cherokee society, enslaved and free, were shaped by the same central Cherokee reality discussed in the first chapter: belonging was lived through kinship, responsibility, and participation.

But here's the hard truth we can't avoid: while Cherokee identity was not originally built on race, the colonial world around us was. And over time, that world pressed in so hard that it reshaped Cherokee law, Cherokee economics, and eventually Cherokee definitions of who counted.

This chapter is about what it looked like before those definitions hardened, when the lines were less about color and more about connection, and how the shift began.

Cherokee Nation in a Changing World

The Cherokee people did not meet Europeans in a peaceful vacuum. Contact brought disease, warfare, trade dependencies, and foreign laws that treated land and human beings as commodities. That world also introduced the Atlantic slave system, one of the most aggressive and profitable machines of dehumanization ever built.

In the Southeast, Africans arrived in growing numbers as a result of European colonization. Some came with colonists as enslaved laborers. Some escaped and formed free communities. Some were captured again. Some were forced into migrations they did not choose. And some found pathways into Native communities, sometimes through refuge and alliance, sometimes through coercion and trade.

Cherokee territory, like the rest of the Southeast, became a crossroads of violence and survival. The story isn't one straight line. It's a tangled set of relationships shaped by external pressure.

That's why it matters to name what many people leave out: long before the Civil War and emancipation, Black people were already living among the Cherokee, some enslaved, some free, some connected by marriage, some connected by shared struggle. Their presence wasn't theoretical. It was real life.

What Cherokee Society Recognized First: Relationships

Before U.S. racial categories spread like a fence line across everything, Cherokee society recognized what it had always recognized first: relationship.

That doesn't mean racism didn't exist. It means it wasn't originally the foundation. When the Cherokee understood identity through clan and community, the most important questions weren't "What are you on paper?" or "What fraction are you?" The questions were practical and social:

- Who claims you?
- Who are your people?
- Who do you live with?
- Who do you answer to?
- Who do you care for?
- Who will stand for you when conflict comes?

This is why the modern habit of treating "Freedmen" as if it equals "outsider" collapses under honest historical study. If belonging is built through living relationships, then the presence of Black people in Cherokee life naturally produced Cherokee-Black families, communities, and identities that cannot be reduced to a label created later.

And this is also where the traditional meaning of "Fullblood" matters again. In Cherokee society, "Fullblood" was about living by Cherokee ways — language, customs, community responsibility. It was never originally a math problem. So, when Black people lived traditionally, raised children in Cherokee life, and participated in the Nation, the real question in a traditional framework wasn't "What are you?" It was "How do you live?"

That truth does not erase the brutality of slavery. It makes history more honest by showing how colonial systems collided with Indigenous systems — and how that collision created lives that don't fit neatly into modern talking points.

Africans, Black Refuge, and the Southeast

Even before removal, the Southeast was full of movement: trade routes, military campaigns, mission networks, intertribal diplomacy, and forced migrations. African people moved through this world too — sometimes fleeing bondage, sometimes captured, sometimes brought by force.

Some Black people sought refuge among Native nations. There were also Native communities pressured to return escapees to white slaveholders and punished when they refused. There were treaties and agreements created by European powers that tried to turn Native nations into border patrols for slavery.

Those pressures mattered. They pushed Indigenous nations into choices that were not made in a clean moral laboratory. They were made under threat of economic, military, and political.

For the Cherokee, the question became: how do you survive as a Nation while surrounded by colonial systems designed to swallow you whole?

Some leaders pursued adaptation. Some resisted. Most did a mixture of both. But as "civilization" policies intensified, mission schools, European-style farming, and written constitutions. The Cherokee Nation was pushed toward a political model that looked more like that of the United States. And embedded in that model was the American racial hierarchy.

Enslavement and the Invasion of Racial Law

Slavery did not begin as a Cherokee institution. It arrived as part of a colonial economy. But over time, slavery did exist within Cherokee society, especially among wealthier families influenced by Southern plantation structures.

This is where people sometimes rush to either excuse it or weaponize it. This book will do neither. The truth is the truth:

- Some Cherokees owned slaves.
- Some Cherokees opposed slavery.
- Some Cherokees benefited from it.
- Some were harmed by the systems built around it.
- And enslaved Black people, like all enslaved people, resisted in every way they could.

The bigger point for this chapter is that slavery brought something beyond forced labor: it brought racial law. And racial law does something different than simple domination. Racial law tries to define identity itself. It tries to declare who is "naturally" above and who is "naturally" below. It turns people into categories.

That's why the spread of slave laws is important historically. It wasn't just about controlling labor. It was about controlling belonging. It was about making Blackness a permanent marker that could override kinship and community.

Once that worldview takes root, society begins to change from the inside out.

Free Blacks, Black Cherokees, and the Reality People Ignore

Not every Black person in Cherokee territory was enslaved. And not every Black person connected to Cherokee society is best described through slavery alone.

Free Black people were living in and around Cherokee communities. Some Black families formed deep ties through marriage and shared community life. There were mixed-ancestry children whose lives were shaped by both worlds. Some people became "Black Cherokee" not as a modern identity trend, but as a lived reality built through home, family, and survival.

And for those who only want the story to be simple, either "they were all enslaved" or "they were all outsiders," that reality is inconvenient.

Because it forces a question: if Cherokee society could recognize belonging through kinship and responsibility, how do you pretend those families weren't Cherokee?

You can't. Not honestly.

What you can do is what the United States often did: replace lived identity with paper identity. Replace community recognition with racial classification. Replace kinship with categories.

And that shift is where the modern fight begins.

Families Are Where History Becomes Real

It's easy to debate identity when you talk in abstractions: "the Nation," "the Freedmen," "citizenship," "rolls." But history lives in families. It lives in kitchens, church benches, work fields, cemeteries, and stories told at reunions. It lives in who raised who, who cared for who, who was buried next to who.

In many Cherokee communities, Black and Cherokee lives intertwined in ways that can't be separated without rewriting reality. People shared neighborhoods. They shared schools at times. They shared labor. They shared worship. They shared hardships. They shared language and customs in some places. They shared the same pressure from white society that sought to control both Indigenous land and Black bodies.

This is also why the later separation on rolls is so violent. It isn't merely bureaucratic. It is an attempt to cut through family history with a pen.

And it worked not completely, but enough to cause lasting harm.

"Fullblood," "Mixed," and the Real Meaning of Those Words

In Chapter 1, we established something most people don't know or pretend not to know: in traditional Cherokee society, "Fullblood" described living by Cherokee ways, not a blood fraction.

That matters here because when colonial racial logic enters the Nation, it starts twisting these terms. It pushes them toward biology and "purity," away from culture and responsibility. It pressures Cherokee society to read identity through the colonizer's eyes.

When you see later arguments that treat "Fullblood" like it means "racially unmixed," you are seeing a colonial rewrite of a Cherokee concept.

Traditional Cherokee society could distinguish between those who lived traditionally and those who lived in more European ways. But that distinction was cultural. It was about language, community practice, and the lifeways people chose — or were pressured — to adopt.

The United States, however, needed an identity to be measurable and enforceable. It needed it to fit into the law. That's where blood quantum would eventually come in, an invented math system designed not to preserve Native people, but to manage them.

The tragedy is that once this framework takes hold, even Cherokee people can begin repeating it as if it were ours.

The Pressure That Set Up the Next Century

By the time removal approached, Cherokee society had already been reshaped by colonial forces. Political factions are formed. Wealth gaps widened. Mission schools have expanded.

Slaveholding has increased in some sectors. And U.S. officials watched all of it, ready to use internal division as leverage.

Meanwhile, Black people in Cherokee territory faced impossible realities: enslaved people living within Cherokee households, free Black people navigating a world designed to criminalize their freedom, and mixed families trying to exist under tightening racial law.

All of this set the stage for what would come next: removal, Indian Territory, the Civil War, emancipation, and the federal labeling of "Freedmen" as a category that would later be turned into a wall.

But before that wall existed, something else existed first: real Cherokee life, where people were known by their relationships and responsibilities.

That is the truth that too many debates try to erase.

What This Chapter Asks the Reader to Accept

If you read this history honestly, you must accept a few things at once:

- Black presence in Cherokee history is not new.
- Black Cherokee identity is not a modern invention.
- Cherokee belonging was not originally built on racial math.
- Slavery brought racial law with it, and that law reshaped Cherokee society.
- Families formed across these lines, and paper later tried to slice them apart.

And once you accept those truths, the modern question changes. It stops being "Why are they claiming Cherokee?" and becomes:

Why was the Nation still repeating a federal system designed to divide us?

That is not a question of abandoning sovereignty. It is a question of practicing sovereignty with integrity.

In the next chapter, we will trace how U.S. influence intensified how "civilization" programs, missionaries, and federal policy pushed Cherokee governance toward written systems that could be measured, regulated, and eventually controlled. Because once the United States could define Cherokee identity on paper, it could begin to decide who counted, and who didn't.

And that decision, more than anything else, is what turned kinship into controversy.

Chapter 3 - When the United States Redefined "Indian"

The Cherokee Nation did not ask the United States to define it.

But the United States never needed an invitation.

From the earliest days of contact, federal policy moved with one consistent purpose: to make Indigenous nations legible to American power. To translate Native life into forms, the U.S. could regulate treaties, borders, property deeds, court systems, and eventually rolls. The language of "civilization" sounded polite enough to some ears, but behind it was a harder truth: if the U.S. could redefine what an "Indian" was, it could control Indian land, limit Indian rights, and ultimately reduce Indian existence to whatever the government needed at the time.

And that is exactly what happened.

This chapter is about that transformation. The moment when Indigenous self-definition began to be overridden by federal definition, and when Cherokee belonging started getting pushed away from kinship and toward categories.

The American Problem with Indigenous Nations

From the U.S. perspective, Native nations were inconvenient.

Not because Native people were unknown. Americans knew exactly who they were dealing with, but because Indigenous nations existed as nations. They had their own governments, laws, diplomacy, territory, and their own ways of defining who belonged.

That kind of sovereignty is a problem for a settler state built on expansion. A country built on taking land cannot tolerate another country sitting on that land, even if that nation predates the United States by centuries. So, the U.S. did what empires do: it created a legal and cultural story that made Indigenous nations seem less legitimate.

Sometimes, that story painted us as "savage" to justify violence. Sometimes, it painted us as "children" to justify control. Sometimes it painted us as "vanishing" to justify theft. But it always served the same end: reducing Indigenous sovereignty.

To reduce a nation, you first reduce how people imagine it. Then you reduce how the law recognizes it.

"Civilization" as Policy: Assimilation with a Smile

In Cherokee history, the word "civilization" appears repeatedly, often as if it were a natural progression, as if the Cherokee simply decided one day to mirror the American South.

But "civilization" was not a cultural trend. It was a federal strategy.

The U.S. government and Christian missionaries pushed Southeastern tribes, including the Cherokee, toward reforms meant to make Native nations easier to absorb. Centralized governments modeled after U.S. structures, written laws,

Christian schooling, European-style farming, private property, and Western gender roles.

Some Cherokee leaders engaged these systems strategically. They believed adaptation might protect the Nation from removal. They believed demonstrating "civilization" might prove to Americans that Cherokee people were capable of self-governance and therefore deserving of respect.

But the U.S. was never offering respect.

It was offering a test that the Cherokee were never meant to pass.

Because even when the Cherokee adopted aspects of the U.S. system, constitutions, courts, and schools, the reward was not security. The reward was tighter control, deeper infiltration, and ultimately removal anyway.

"Civilization" was a trap dressed as an opportunity.

The Shift from Community Recognition to Legal Recognition

Once identity becomes a legal matter, it starts to change.

In a kinship-based society, belonging is affirmed by relationships: family, clan, community participation, and shared responsibility. In legal society, belonging is affirmed by systems: documents, courts, registries, and definitions written down by authorities.

As Cherokee governance became more formal, partly by internal choice, partly by external pressure. The Nation had to translate its values into laws that could be enforced consistently. That is not inherently wrong. Nations codify rules. Governments organize themselves. But the danger comes when the form begins to replace the spirit, and when outside pressure determines what the "proper" form should be.

Federal involvement pushed Cherokee life toward a model the U.S. recognized as "real government." The cost was that Cherokee identity, once relational, became increasingly vulnerable to being treated like a status granted by legal machinery.

This is where the battle lines of the future begin. When belonging becomes dependent on a system that can be manipulated, the people most vulnerable to manipulation are the ones already treated as marginal.

And in America, Blackness was always treated as marginal.

Race Enters Through Law, Not Just Attitude

It is tempting to treat racism as a personal failing, something that lives in individual hearts. But racism becomes powerful when it becomes law.

The American racial order was not an accident of feelings. It was built through policy: slave codes, property law, court decisions, census categories, and the constant legal invention of "whiteness" as entitlement.

As the Cherokee Nation was pressured to adopt American-style legal structures, American-style racial thinking came with it. That doesn't mean Cherokee culture suddenly became identical to white Southern culture. It means the Nation was being reshaped inside a world where race determined freedom, labor, and rights.

Slavery intensified that process. Slaveholding required legal definitions: who could be enslaved, what status children inherited, what punishment was permitted, who could testify in court, who had the right to own property, and who could move freely.

These questions force society to draw lines.

And once you draw lines around Blackness, those lines tend to harden.

Over time, Cherokee law began to reflect more of the surrounding racial logic, not because it was Cherokee at the root, but because it was the dominant system pressing in on all sides.

"Indian" as a Federal Category

The United States did something subtle and deadly: it turned "Indian" into a federal category.

That category was never simply descriptive. It was administrative. It existed to manage a population the government intended to control and eventually assimilate. And like all administrative categories, it requires boundaries. It requires definitions. It required rules that could be applied in offices and courtrooms by people who didn't know the communities they were defining.

Once the government needs a category, it needs a method of measurement. And measurement demands simplification.

The Cherokee Nation had its own understanding of belonging. But the U.S. needed a system that fit federal needs: land distribution, treaty enforcement when convenient, removal when convenient, and later allotment.

That is why U.S. systems repeatedly tried to answer the question: "Who is an Indian?"

Not to honor Native identity, but to regulate it.

The Deep Problem: Paper Can Be Weaponized

The more Cherokee life became entangled with U.S. paperwork, the more identity could be altered with a pen.

A kinship network can be attacked, but it is difficult to rewrite. A family knows who they are. A community knows who belongs. A clan system carries memory.

Paper, however, can be edited. Paper can be misfiled. Paper can be "corrected." Paper can be divided into categories that create social reality over time, even when those categories are false to begin with.

And once paper becomes authority, the people who control the paper control the story.

This is why the latter roll-era divisions are not just "records." They are acts of power.

It is also why debates today that rely solely on paperwork — without understanding the colonial purpose behind that paperwork — are debates happening inside a trap.

The Cherokee Nation's Impossible Choices

It would be easy to tell this chapter as a clean moral story: the U.S. imposed, the Cherokee resisted, end of the discussion. But history is not neat.

Cherokee leaders faced impossible choices. The Nation was under constant threat, military, economic, and territorial. Federal and state officials used pressure, promises, and violence interchangeably. Some Cherokees believed adopting U.S. forms might protect the Nation. Others believed it would destroy us from within. Many were simply trying to survive.

Those internal debates about tradition, adaptation, leadership, land, and sovereignty shaped Cherokee politics for generations.

They also shaped how the Nation would later confront questions about slavery, emancipation, and citizenship.

Because once the U.S. model becomes the model everyone must speak, even Cherokee arguments can begin sounding like U.S. arguments.

That is how colonization reproduces itself.

Why This Chapter Matters for Freedmen History

Cherokee Freedmen history is often treated like it begins in 1866, or begins with a roll category, or begins in a courtroom.

It doesn't.

It begins with this larger transformation: the steady replacement of Indigenous self-definition with federal definition. The steady pressure to reduce belonging to categories that the U.S. could manage. The steady tightening of race as a tool for sorting human beings into rights and non-rights.

When the United States later labeled people "Freedmen" inside Native nations, it was not inventing a neutral term. It was expanding a long-running project: using administrative categories to control Native governance and remake Native identity.

That project required division. And racial division is one of the most efficient tools colonization has ever used.

The tragedy is not only what the U.S. did. The tragedy is how effective it was at forcing Native nations to argue about ourselves using the colonizer's measuring stick.

That is why this history must begin before the rolls.

Because the rolls were not the beginning.
They were payoffs.

Moving Forward

In the next section of this book, we widen the lens and talk directly about slavery, not only African chattel slavery, but the broader history of enslavement on this continent, including the enslavement of Native Americans by European colonists. That context matters because it reveals something the record debates often try to hide:

Slavery in Indian Country did not arise in a vacuum. It emerged inside a colonial system designed to commodify human beings and dismantle nations.

And once you understand how that system worked, you can better understand how the term "Freedman" became more than a description of emancipation.

It became a weaponized category one that would later be used to challenge Cherokee belonging itself.

But the deeper question remains:

If Cherokee identity existed before the United States defined it, then why are we still letting federal categories tell us who we are?

Chapter 4 - A Brief History of Slavery in America

If we're going to speak honestly about Cherokee Freedmen, we must speak honestly about the system that produced the very word "Freedman" in the first place. That system wasn't created in Indian Country. It was created through colonization. And it reshaped every community it touched, Native, Black, and white, by turning human beings into property and then building law, economy, and identity on top of that theft.

This chapter is not meant to be exhaustive. Entire libraries exist on the history of slavery in America. But we need a clear foundation — one that explains what slavery became in the United States, why it hardened into a racial caste system, and how those ideas later spilled into Native nations and federal Indian policy.

Because when people argue today as if "Freedman" is merely a label on an old roll, they are pretending it wasn't born from one of the most powerful legal machines ever constructed: the American system of racial slavery.

Slavery Didn't Begin in 1619, But a System Did

Most people have heard a single date repeated so often it becomes the whole story: 1619. That year matters, but it is not the beginning of slavery in the Americas. Europeans were already enslaving people across the Caribbean, Central America, and South America long before English colonies stabilized in what would become the United States. And Europeans were already enslaving Native Americans on this continent even earlier.

What 1619 represents is the early formation of an English colonial system that would grow into a permanent economy built on bondage. As English colonies expanded, they didn't just rely on enslaved labor. They developed laws that made enslaved status inheritable, permanent, and tied to race.

That is the turning point we must understand. The evil of American slavery wasn't only its violence, though the violence was constant. The deeper evil was how slavery was engineered into law so completely that generations could be born into captivity and treated as a natural category of human life.

From Indentured Servitude to Racialized Chattel Slavery

In the earliest colonial period, labor systems in the English colonies were mixed. Indentured servitude existed — people bound to labor for a set number of years, sometimes under brutal conditions. Africans were present in this world too, and early on, the boundaries between indenture and slavery were not always fixed in the way they later became.

But the colonies wanted something more profitable and more controllable: permanent labor.

Over time, colonial legislatures created a system where Africans and their descendants were legally transformed into chattel movable property. Unlike indenture, this status had no end date. Unlike other forms of bondage seen in various societies across history, American chattel slavery was increasingly defined by two brutal principles:

- Permanent ownership (enslavement for life)

- Hereditary status (children inheriting slavery through the mother)

That second point is critical. When slavery becomes hereditary, it becomes self-reproducing. A slaveholder doesn't just purchase labor; they purchase the future.

And once slavery becomes hereditary, controlling women's bodies becomes part of the system. Sexual violence becomes not just abuse — it becomes an economic strategy. Families become targets. Lineage becomes a battlefield.

This is not a side detail. This is the engine room for the system.

Law Made Race into a Cage

American slavery didn't survive because people were simply "racist." It survived because the law made racism profitable and enforceable.

Colonial and later state laws built a world where Blackness was treated as a legal marker that determined:

- who could be owned
- who could testify in court
- who could legally marry
- who could travel without papers
- whether children would be free or enslaved
- who could own property
- who could be punished without limits

Over time, the colonies — and later the states — hardened the idea that Africans and their descendants were a separate class of human beings, naturally suited for bondage. This wasn't just a prejudice. It was a political and economic invention designed to protect wealth built on stolen labor.

And it wasn't only aimed at Black people. This framework also created "whiteness" as a legal advantage. Poor Europeans could be kept invested in the system by giving them status above enslaved Africans, even if they had little wealth of their own. Divide people by race, and you can unite them under the banner of hierarchy.

That same strategy would later be used against Native nations in different forms, divide communities, separate people into categories, and then use the categories to control land and rights.

Slavery as an Economy, Not Just a Crime

When people talk about slavery as if it were only "a moral failing," they can unknowingly soften what it really was: an economic system.

Slavery was not random cruelty. It was an organized extraction.

Enslaved people cleared land, built infrastructure, produced crops, and created wealth that fueled colonial growth and, later, the expansion of the United States. By the time the cotton economy exploded, slavery was tied to banking, insurance, shipping, and global trade. Human bodies became collateral. Enslaved people were mortgaged, leased, insured, inherited, and seized.

This is why slavery's legacy doesn't end with emancipation. When a country builds wealth through stolen labor for generations, that wealth doesn't disappear when the law changes. It transfers. It compounds. It becomes "normal."

And the people whose labor was stolen are expected to begin freedom with nothing.

Resistance Was Constant

Another lie that survives is the idea that enslaved people were passive until a few famous revolts happened. The truth is that resistance was constant because human beings resist dehumanization as naturally as they breathe.

Resistance took many forms:

- escaping when possible
- sabotaging tools and production
- learning to read despite punishment
- preserving language, song, faith, and family structure under assault
- creating networks of support and information
- negotiating for small spaces of autonomy
- fighting back in ways that rarely made it into official records

This matters for our story because when we later discuss slavery in Indian Country, we are not discussing a different species of enslavement with different human realities. Enslaved people in Cherokee society resisted, too, because they were human too.

And the strategies they used, survival, refusal, endurance, and escape, are part of the foundation of Freedmen history.

The Civil War Didn't Begin Over "States' Rights" in the Abstract

It is common to hear the Civil War described as a conflict about "states' rights." The question is: states' rights to do what?

The answer is not complicated. The central issue was slavery, its expansion, its protection, and the political power it gave to those who benefited from it. By the mid-1800s, the United States was locked in a struggle over whether slavery would spread into new territories and states, and whether the nation would continue expanding as a slave empire.

This is where we must be clear: slavery wasn't a side issue that accidentally caused a war. Slavery was the economic and political foundation for a powerful segment of the country. When that foundation was threatened, war followed.

But the Civil War's impact goes beyond battlefields. It triggered massive changes in law, citizenship, and federal power. Those changes would reach into Indian Territory and would directly shape the treaties and categories that later defined Freedmen status in Native nations.

Emancipation Was Not a Finish Line

The end of slavery in law did not end slavery's logic.

Emancipation did not come with land, wealth, safety, or equality. It came with a new fight: the fight to survive freedom in a society that had built itself on Black unfreedom.

After the war, southern states and local governments moved quickly to recreate control through new mechanisms, such as Black Codes, convict leasing, vagrant laws, racial terror, and economic dependence through sharecropping and debt. The law changed, but the appetite for domination did not.

The United States promised freedom, then allowed systems to emerge that criminalized Black life and exploited Black labor under new names.

And here is where the term "Freedman" becomes more than a dictionary definition. In federal language, it described a person freed from slavery. It often meant freedom in theory, targeted in practice, and forced to fight for rights that should have been automatic.

That tension between promised citizenship and denied citizenship will mirror what happens in Native nations after emancipation, including the Cherokee Nation.

Why This Chapter Belongs in a Book About Cherokee Freedmen

Some readers may wonder why a book about Cherokee Freedmen spends time on the broader history of slavery in America. The reason is simple:

The Cherokee Freedmen story sits at the intersection of two American projects:

- the enslavement of African people and the creation of racial caste
Some readers may wonder why a book about Cherokee Freedmen spends time on the broader history of slavery in America. The reason is simple:

The Cherokee Freedmen story sits at the intersection of two American projects:

- the enslavement of African people and the creation of racial caste
- the colonization of Indigenous nations and the management of Native sovereignty

When these projects collided in Indian Country, the result was not just "slavery among Cherokees." The result was a complex history of Black life inside a Native nation, shaped by both Cherokee community realities and U.S. racial politics.

If you do not understand how American law turned Blackness into a legal cage, you will misunderstand why federal categories like "Freedman" became so powerful later. If you do not understand how slavery's logic survived emancipation, you will misunderstand why legal promises made in treaties were later undermined, ignored, or reinterpreted.

This is not ancient history. These structures still echo today — in who is believed, who is questioned, who is required to prove belonging, and who is treated as if they should be grateful for rights guaranteed by law.

Why This History Matters for Indian Country

Slavery in America was not just a Southern institution. It was a national institution, one that shaped federal policy, federal courts, and federal attitudes toward race, citizenship, and land. Those same attitudes shaped how the United States interacted with Native nations.

When the U.S. government negotiated treaties, enforced removal, created the Dawes Rolls, and later imposed blood quantum, it did so inside a worldview already structured by racial hierarchy. That worldview did not stay confined to white society. It seeped into Native nations through law, economics, missionary influence, and federal pressure.

Understanding that context matters because it reveals something many people try to avoid:

The racial categories used to divide Cherokee citizens were not Cherokee inventions. They were American inventions.

And once those categories entered Cherokee law, they created divisions that had never existed in traditional Cherokee society.

The Collision of Two Systems

When African slavery and Indigenous sovereignty collided, neither system remained untouched. Black people living in Cherokee territory, enslaved, free, or somewhere in between, were shaped by Cherokee community life and by U.S. racial law. Cherokee society was shaped by its own traditions and by the colonial systems pressing in on all sides.

This collision produced:

- Black Cherokees
- enslaved Africans living in Cherokee households

- free Black families connected to Cherokee communities
- mixed-ancestry children navigating two worlds
- Cherokee citizens influenced by U.S. racial thinking
- federal agents determined to divide Native nations by race

None of this history fits neatly into modern talking points. It is messy, human, and shaped by survival.

But if you ignore that complexity, you cannot understand why the term "Freedman" became so powerful or so weaponized in later federal policy.

The Road Toward Indian Territory

By the time the Cherokee Nation was forced west, the United States had already built a racial system that defined Blackness as property and whiteness as privilege. That system traveled with the federal government into every treaty negotiation, every removal policy, and every legal decision involving Native nations.

When the Cherokee were forced to rebuild in Indian Territory, they did so inside a world already shaped by racial hierarchy. Black people were part of that world as laborers, as family members, as community members, as survivors of a system that treated them as commodities.

And the United States was watching all of it, ready to use racial categories as tools of control.

The Legacy That Sets Up the Next Chapter

Before we can talk about slavery in Indian Country, and before we can discuss Cherokee Freedmen specifically. We must understand the system that shaped the world, which both Black and Native people were forced to navigate.

Because the term "Freedman" did not fall from the sky.

It was born from a legal system designed to:

- control Black bodies
- control Native land
- control citizenship
- control sovereignty

And once the United States created that system, it carried those tools into every interaction with Native nations.

In the next chapter, we narrow the lens and confront a truth often left out entirely: slavery on this continent did not begin with Africans alone. Native Americans were enslaved by European colonists long before African chattel slavery took root. That system destabilized Indigenous societies across the Southeast and laid the groundwork for the racial hierarchy that would later shape Cherokee law, Cherokee politics, and Cherokee belonging.

Because once you understand how colonization used slavery to divide and control, you start seeing the pattern everywhere, including in the fight over Cherokee Freedmen.

Chapter 5 - Slavery in Indian Country

If you only tell the story of slavery in Indian Country beginning with Native slaveholding, you end up with a history that feels upside down. You end up treating Native nations as the starting point of a system that was already centuries old by the time it reached us in its most profitable form.

That version of the story is convenient for the United States. It trims colonial responsibility down to a footnote and turns Native nations into the main stage. It also creates a false moral simplicity, either to weaponize shame against Native people or to excuse everything by claiming we were merely copying.

Neither is it honest.

The truth is more difficult, and more important: Native people were among the first enslaved peoples in what became the United States. Europeans enslaved Indigenous men, women, and children from the earliest period of colonization. They built an economy of captivity alongside the theft of land. They used slavery not just as labor, but as a strategy, a way to destabilize nations, encourage warfare, and break resistance.

Only after that long history of imposed violence did slavery become something some Native nations participated in, under pressure and within a colonial world that rewarded imitation and punished refusal.

To understand Cherokee Freedmen, we must understand that full arc.

Enslaved Before "Slavery" Became a Southern Identity

When people imagine slavery, many picture cotton fields and plantations in the Deep South. That image is real, but it is not the beginning. The earliest slavery in the Americas included Indigenous slavery — Native people taken, sold, transported, and forced into labor in missions, mines, households, farms, and colonial settlements.

This was not occasional. In many places, it was foundational.

European powers treated Native bodies as resources in the same way they treated Native land as a resource. They captured people during raids, demanded captives as tribute, purchased captives from rival groups, and used legal fiction to justify it all. They baptized Native captives and called it "conversion." They claimed Native people were "prisoners of war" and called it "order." They labeled forced labor as "service" to make it sound less like theft.

But it was a theft. And it was slavery.

And in the Southeast, it grew into an industry.

The Indian Slave Trade: A Market Built on Destabilization

In the Southeast, European colonies developed a brutal trade in Native captives. Indigenous people were taken from their communities and sold as labor not only locally, but often out of the region entirely, shipped to the Caribbean or other colonies where escape was harder and where the buyer had no ties to the captives' homeland.

This wasn't accidental. It served a purpose.

European colonists understood something: the easiest way to defeat a nation is to fracture it. Encourage conflict. And rewards raids. Buy captives. Turn neighbors into enemies. Turn survival into competition. Then step back and claim Indigenous people are "naturally violent," as if the violence was not being financed and directed.

Colonial powers used trade goods, weapons, and economic dependence to fuel this system. Captives became currency. Raiding became an incentive. Communities were weakened from within, and then colonists blamed Native instability as the reason they "had" to take more control.

This is what the empire does: it creates chaos and then sells itself as the solution.

For Cherokee communities living in this world, the constant pressure was not theoretical. It was a daily reality of raids, shifting alliances, threats from neighboring groups forced into motion, and colonists manipulated those conflicts for advantage.

And while the Cherokee are not the only people in this story, the lesson applies directly: slavery was introduced to Indigenous life through colonial force and colonial markets.

Why Indigenous Slavery Declined And African Slavery Expanded

Over time, colonial economies shifted toward enslaving Africans on an increasing scale. The shift did not happen because Europeans "learned" that Indigenous slavery was wrong. It happened because colonial powers calculated that African slavery was more profitable and easier to control.

Native people had deep knowledge of the land. Escaping was often more possible. Communities sometimes mount rescue or retaliation efforts. And epidemics devastated Indigenous populations, reducing the labor pool that colonists were trying to exploit.

Colonists responded by importing people who were ripped from their homelands, languages, and kin networks with fewer pathways to return, and who could be racialized into a permanent caste. The law followed the money: Blackness became a legal container for bondage.

This is the hard truth: the rise of African chattel slavery did not replace Indigenous suffering — it expanded the machinery of suffering, refining it into a system that could reproduce itself.

By the time slavery reached its height in the American South, it was already a sophisticated legal technology. It came with paperwork, courts, patrols, and a story that claimed Black people were naturally meant for captivity.

That story did not stay in white communities. It spreads outward like poison.

How the Colonial World Pressured Native Nations

By the early 1800s, Cherokee territory sat beside and increasingly inside a Southern economy driven by slavery, private property, and plantation wealth. The United States and surrounding states didn't just want Cherokee land. They wanted Cherokee society to become predictable and exploitable.

That's where the "civilization" strategy shows up again. The Cherokee were pressured to adopt:

- private land ownership
- centralized government systems legible to U.S. law
- Christian schooling
- plantation-style agriculture

- and, in some cases, the labor systems that supported plantation wealth

The pressure was not only ideological. It was economic and political. Trading relationships rewarded certain practices. Diplomatic recognition favored leaders who could operate in American legal language. With wealth accumulated in ways that mirrored the surrounding South.

Within that world, slavery could become a tool of upward mobility for a small segment of Cherokee society, especially those already positioned to benefit from American-style property systems.

This is where the story becomes uncomfortable but necessary: some Cherokees owned enslaved Africans. Not as an abstract "influence," but as a lived practice. And that practice brought the racial logic of the slave South deeper into Cherokee law and daily life.

But we must be precise here.

Cherokee involvement in slavery did not mean Cherokee society was identical to white Southern society. It did not mean all the Cherokees participated. It did not mean all Cherokees agreed. It did mean that a colonial system succeeded in pushing parts of Cherokee life toward the surrounding economy, and that shift had consequences that would echo for generations.

Slavery in Cherokee Society: Not Monolithic

One of the most dishonest habits in this subject is speaking as if "the Cherokee" did one thing, believed one thing, and benefited in one way. Cherokee society, like any society, has divisions — class divisions, political divisions, geographic divisions, and cultural divisions.

Some Cherokee families held enslaved people and adopted plantation practices. Some did not. Some Cherokee people lived traditionally, resisting assimilation and resisting the economic reshaping of Cherokee life. Some Cherokee communities became more entwined with U.S. trade and legal systems. Some actively opposed those changes.

And within all of this, enslaved Black people were not passive objects. They were human beings living inside a violent structure, and they acted like human beings act: they resisted, endured, negotiated, escaped, when possible, protected family, preserved identity, and fought for space to breathe.

The presence of slavery created a layered Cherokee reality:

- a Cherokee Nation under threat from U.S. expansion
- Cherokee leaders are trying different strategies of survival
- Cherokee wealth and class stratification are increasing
- Black life inside Cherokee territory is shaped by both Cherokee society and the American racial regime

That layered reality is exactly why the term "Freedman" later becomes so loaded. It isn't just about emancipation. It is about where Black people stood inside a Native nation, at the moment the U.S. decided to impose new categories.

Removal Carried Slavery into Indian Territory

When the Cherokee were forced from their homelands, the trauma did not travel alone. Removal carried slavery into Indian Territory. Enslaved Black people were marched west alongside the Cherokee, suffering the same exposure and brutality of displacement while still being denied freedom.

This point matters because it destroys another convenient myth — that slavery was something happening "over there" in the South, and Indian Territory was somehow separate.

It wasn't separate. It was connected.

Indian Territory became a place where the United States relocated Native nations while still ensuring the surrounding American order, race hierarchy, property obsession, and political manipulation continued to shape our lives. Removal did not remove the Cherokee from American pressure. It brought that pressure to the West.

And it brought enslaved people to the West, too.

So, when we speak about the roots of Cherokee Freedmen, we are speaking about families and communities forged in forced migration, shaped by Cherokee society, and targeted by U.S. racial systems all at once.

Shared Trauma, Different Positions

Here is one of the most important truths in this chapter, and it must be handled carefully:

Native people and Black people experienced colonial America through different forms of violence, but those violences were connected.

Native nations faced land theft, removal, forced assimilation, and repeated attempts at national destruction. Black people faced chattel slavery, hereditary bondage, and racial caste enforced through law and terror. These are not identical experiences. They should not collapse into one story.

But they are connected because colonial systems needed two outcomes:

- Indigenous land opened for settlement
- Black labor was exploited to build wealth on that stolen land

That is the design underneath the chaos.

In Indian Country, those designs collided. Black lives existed inside Native nations. Native nations were pressured to adopt American economic structures. The U.S. manipulated both realities to expand its power.

And out of that collision came Black Cherokee people who were not simply "slaves of Cherokees," but human beings whose lives, families, and identities formed inside Cherokee society, in a world that tried to control everyone.

What This Chapter Leaves Us With

At the end of this chapter, a few truths should be clear:

- Europeans enslaved Native Americans from the earliest period of colonization.
- The Indian slave trade destabilized Indigenous nations as a strategy of empire.
- African chattel slavery expanded because it was more profitable and easier to enforce.
- U.S. "civilization" pressure reshaped Native economies and governance.
- Slavery existed within Cherokee society, but Cherokee society was never monolithic.
- Removal carried slavery into Indian Territory, setting the stage for the next era.

And that next era is where the word "Freedman" begins to take legal shape.

Because when the Civil War arrives in Indian Territory, it doesn't arrive as a distant conflict. It arrives as a storm that forces every nation, every community, and every family to confront the future: What does freedom mean? Who gets to claim it? And who decides?

In the next chapter, we turn directly toward that collision toward the Civil War in Indian Territory, the fracture inside the

Cherokee Nation, and the road toward emancipation and treaty citizenship.

Chapter 6 - Cherokee Slaveholders and Cherokee Resistance

The Civil War didn't just arrive in Indian Territory. It cracked open every tension the Cherokee Nation had been carrying for decades. Slavery, assimilation, land, sovereignty, identity, survival. All of it collided at once. And the United States, as always, was ready to use those fractures to its advantage.

But before we step fully into the war, we need to understand the landscape the Cherokee Nation was standing on. Because the choices made during the Civil War didn't come out of nowhere. They were shaped by everything this chapter has laid out: class divisions, cultural divides, colonial pressure, and the presence of enslaved and free Black people whose lives were intertwined with Cherokee life long before the first shot was fired.

The Cherokee Nation Was Already Divided Before the First Battle

By the 1850s, the Cherokee Nation was not a unified political body. It was a nation still healing from removal, still rebuilding its government, still negotiating its identity in a world that demanded it become more "American" to survive.

Inside that world:

- wealthy Cherokee slaveholders leaned toward the Confederacy
- traditional Cherokee communities leaned toward neutrality or the Union
- mixed families and border communities tried to avoid the conflict entirely
- enslaved Black people watched closely, knowing their future depended on the outcome

The United States understood these divisions. So did the Confederacy. Both sides courted Cherokee leaders, promising protection, recognition, and political advantage. Both sides wanted Native nations as allies. Not because they cared about Native sovereignty, but because they cared about Native land and Native strategic value.

And the Cherokee Nation was caught in the middle.

Why Some Cherokee Leaders Chose the Confederacy

It is easy to flatten this history into a single accusation:
"Cherokees joined the Confederacy because they supported slavery."

The truth is more complicated and more revealing.

Some Cherokee leaders aligned with the Confederacy because:

- They feared the United States after the removal
- They believed the Confederacy would respect Cherokee sovereignty more
- They had economic ties to Southern markets

- They owned enslaved people and wanted to protect that wealth
- They believed neutrality was impossible

None of these reasons excuses the choice. But they explained it.

And they show how deeply colonial pressure had reshaped Cherokee political life.

Why Other Cherokees Chose the Union. Or Chose Neither Side.

Many Cherokee people, especially traditionalists, poorer families, and communities farther from plantation wealth, did not want to join the Confederacy. Some opposed slavery outright. Some opposed aligning with a government built on racial hierarchy. Some simply wanted to avoid another war forced on them by outsiders.

Others believed the United States, despite its violence, was the only path toward long-term survival.

And many Cherokee people, especially those who had endured the worst of removal, wanted nothing to do with either side. They had already seen what American wars did to Native nations.

But neutrality was not an option for the United States, nor did the Confederacy intend to allow.

Black Cherokees Faced a Different War Entirely

For enslaved Black people in Cherokee territory, the Civil War was not a political debate. It was a question of life, death, and freedom.

They watched:

- which Cherokee leaders aligned with the Confederacy
- which communities resisted
- which families offered refuge
- Which routes might lead to Union lines
- Which promises might lead to citizenship after the war?

Black Cherokees were not passive observers. They were strategists. They were survivors. They were people navigating a war inside a nation that had not yet decided whether they would be citizens or outsiders once freedom came.

Their choices: escape, alliance, resistance, endurance, shaped the war in Indian Territory just as much as the choices of Cherokee leaders.

The Civil War Would Force the Cherokee Nation to Choose

By 1861, the Cherokee Nation was split:

- Principal Chief John Ross initially tried to keep the Nation neutral
- Stand Watie and other pro-Confederate leaders pushed for an alliance with the South
- traditional communities resisted Confederate influence
- enslaved and free Black people watched for any path toward liberation

The United States and the Confederacy both demanded loyalty. Both threatened consequences. Both promised protection that they had no intention of honoring.

And under that pressure, the Cherokee Nation fractured.

Some Cherokee regiments fought for the Confederacy.
Some fought for the Union.
Some communities fought only to protect themselves.

And enslaved Black people in Cherokee households, in Cherokee communities, in Cherokee territory, seized whatever opportunities the chaos created.

Some escaped to Union forts.
Some joined Union regiments.
Some stayed close to Cherokee families who protected them.
Some were forced deeper into Confederate territory.
Some resisted from within.

Their actions were not footnotes. They were part of the war.

Why This Chapter Matters for What Comes Next

The Civil War in Indian Territory was not simply a conflict between North and South. It was a conflict inside the Cherokee Nation, a conflict shaped by slavery, sovereignty, survival, and the long shadow of colonial pressure.

And when the war ended, the United States would use that conflict to impose something new:

The Treaty of 1866 was the document that created the legal category "Freedmen" within the Cherokee Nation.

That treaty did not fall from the sky.
It was born from everything this chapter has described:

- Cherokee slaveholding
- Cherokee resistance
- Black resistance
- internal divisions
- external manipulation
- and a war that forced every community to choose a side

In the next chapter, we step directly into that moment, the Civil War in Indian Territory, the choices Cherokee leaders made, the choices Black Cherokees made, and the road toward emancipation and treaty citizenship that would reshape the Nation forever.

Chapter 7 - What Does "Freedman" Mean?

The word "Freedman" did not create Cherokee history.
But it has shaped how that history has been interpreted, manipulated, and weaponized.

And that is why understanding the term matters — not as a dictionary entry, but as a political tool that reshaped lives.

The Federal Logic Behind the Label

When the United States applied the term "Freedmen" to Native nations, it was not simply describing a group of people. It was creating a category that the federal government could use to:

- monitor Native nations
- enforce treaty obligations
- reshape tribal citizenship
- justify intervention
- and eventually justify allotment

The label was a foothold, a way for the U.S. to insert itself into internal Native affairs under the guise of protecting formerly enslaved people.

But the federal government was not protecting Black people out of moral clarity. It was protecting its own interests.

If the U.S. could define who counted as a citizen inside Native nations, it could weaken Native sovereignty from within. And if it could divide Native nations into categories: "by blood," "by status," "Freedmen," "intermarried whites." It could fracture the political unity that made Native nations harder to control.

The Freedmen category was one of the earliest tools in that strategy.

The Cherokee Nation Was Not the Only Target

It's important to remember that the Cherokee Nation was not singled out. The United States imposed similar treaty requirements on the Creek, Seminole, Choctaw, and Chickasaw Nations. In each case, the federal government used the Freedmen category to:

- force emancipation
- force citizenship debates
- force internal restructuring
- and force Native nations into closer dependence on federal oversight

The pattern was the same everywhere:
freedom with strings attached.

And those strings were tied to federal power.

The Word "Freedman" Became a Legal Boundary, not a Cultural One

Inside the Cherokee Nation, the term "Freedman" did not describe a cultural identity. It described a legal status created by the federal government and enforced through treaty law.

But over time, that legal status hardened into a social boundary. Not because Cherokee tradition demanded it, but because federal systems rewarded it.

Rolls, allotment records, census categories, and court decisions all reinforced the idea that "Freedmen" were a separate class of people. And once the paperwork created that separation, people began to treat it as if it reflected cultural truth.

This is how colonial categories become inherited beliefs.

This is how a federal label becomes a social wall.

This is how temporary legal status becomes a permanent political argument.

The Consequences of a Category

Once the Freedmen category existed, it shaped everything that came after:

- who received land
- who received payments
- who was counted as a citizen
- who was excluded
- who had political power
- who was vulnerable to removal or disenfranchisement

And because the category was racialized, tied to Blackness, tied to slavery, tied to federal oversight. It became a pressure point inside Native nations.

The U.S. knew exactly what it was doing.

Divide a nation by race, and you weaken its sovereignty.
Divide a nation by paperwork, and you weaken its unity.
Divide a nation into categories, and you can control its future.

Why the Word Still Matters Today

In the Cherokee Nation today, the word "Freedman" is still used in ways that echo federal intentions more than the Cherokee tradition. It is still used to:

- question belonging
- justify exclusion
- frame Black Cherokees as outsiders
- and reduce complex family history to a single legal label

But the truth is simple:

Freedmen's descendants are Cherokee.
Not because of the federal category.
Not because of a roll.
Not because of a treaty.
But because their families lived, labored, worshiped, suffered, survived, and belonged inside the Cherokee Nation long before the United States decided to put a name on them.

The category "Freedman" did not create Black Cherokees.
It tried to contain them.

What Comes Next

Now we've defined the word and exposed the political machinery behind it. We can move into the moment when the term became unavoidable: the Civil War in Indian Territory.

Because the Civil War did not just end slavery.
It forced the Cherokee Nation to confront questions that had been building for decades:

- Who are we?
- Who belongs to it?
- What does freedom mean inside a Native nation?
- And who gets to decide?

In the next chapter, we step into that conflict into the alliances, betrayals, survival strategies, and federal pressures that shaped the Treaty of 1866 and the future of Cherokee citizenship.

And we will see, clearly, how the word "Freedman" became a turning point not only for Black Cherokees, but for the Cherokee Nation itself.

Chapter 8 - The Civil War in Indian Territory

The Civil War is often taught as if it happened somewhere else, Virginia battlefields, Mississippi river towns, and Washington politics. Indian Territory is treated like a side note, if it's mentioned at all. But for the Cherokee Nation, the war was not distant. It was not abstract. It was a crisis that struck the Nation's already-fractured foundation and forced every community to make choices under threat.

And for Black people living in Cherokee society, enslaved, free, and those already living as Black Cherokees, the war was not simply "politics." It was the difference between bondage and freedom, between family separation and family survival, between being counted as property and being recognized as a person.

This chapter is about that collision: a war that reached into Indian Territory and exposed the divisions that removal, class, and slavery had already deepened.

A Nation Already Divided Before the First Shot

By the time the Civil War began, the Cherokee Nation was still living with the trauma of removal. Communities were rebuilt. Leadership has been contested. Relationships with the United States were strained and unstable. Economic divisions were sharpening, and slavery present within parts of the Nation had tied some Cherokee citizens to the Southern economy.

These weren't just disagreements. They were competing for visions of what the Cherokee Nation should become.

Some Cherokee citizens saw alignment with Southern interests as practical survival. The surrounding world was slaveholding. The markets were Southern. Political connections were Southern. The U.S. government had already shown it could not be trusted, and many believed that if war was coming, the Confederacy might offer a better deal or at least a chance to preserve autonomy.

Others believed aligning with a rebellion built on slavery would betray Cherokee values and deepen the Nation's dependence on a system designed to dominate. Some opposed the Confederacy on principle. Some opposed it for strategic reasons. Some simply wanted to avoid the war entirely.

And then some had no choice in any of these calculations: enslaved people.

For them, the question wasn't which political alliance protected sovereignty. The question was: Will this war finally break the chains?

Why Indian Territory Mattered to Both Sides

Indian Territory mattered in the Civil War for several reasons:

- Geography: It sat as a corridor between the Confederacy and the West.
- Resources: Livestock, crops, and trade routes were valuable to armies.
- Politics: Both sides wanted alliances with Native nations to claim legitimacy and manpower.
- Control: Whoever controlled Indian Territory could threaten supply lines and influence surrounding regions.

This meant Native nations were pressured, recruited, threatened, and manipulated again. The Cherokee Nation was forced into a choice where no outcome was clean.

The United States, after decades of removal and broken promises, expected loyalty. The Confederacy offered recognition and negotiation while also being built explicitly to protect slavery.

That is the cruel position colonization creates: forcing a nation to choose between powers that both see it as an asset rather than as a fully respected sovereign.

Cherokee Alignment Was Not a Single Decision

It is important to understand that Cherokee involvement in the Civil War cannot be reduced to "the Cherokee chose the Confederacy" or "the Cherokee chose the Union." Cherokee communities did not move as a single body. They moved in factions, often shaped by:

- geography
- class
- leadership loyalties
- survival calculations based on proximity to military force

Some Cherokee citizens served Confederate units. Some served as Union forces. Some switched sides. Some tried to stay neutral and were punished for it. Some were forced into roles by occupying armies.

War doesn't respect nuance, but history must.

And in the middle of it all, Black people, especially enslaved Black people, were treated as military assets, labor sources, and bargaining chips.

Black Cherokees and Enslaved People in a War Zone

For enslaved Black people in Cherokee society, war created danger and opportunity at the same time.

Danger, because war often meant:

- forced labor for military units
- increased surveillance and punishment
- family separation as people were moved for "safety" or strategy
- chaos that allowed kidnapping, re-enslavement, or violence without accountability

Opportunity, because war disrupted the system that maintained slavery.

When armies moved through an area, enslaved people watched for openings: a chance to flee, to hide, to reach Union lines, to negotiate with local authorities, to protect family, to gather information. In the wider South, the Civil War created what historians often describe as self-emancipation, enslaved people forcing the issue of freedom by leaving plantations and making slavery unworkable.

That dynamic existed in Indian Territory, too, though under different conditions and with different dangers.

The war created movement. And movement created possibilities.

For free Black people and Black Cherokees already living in communities, the war threatened to erase fragile freedoms. Accusations, violence, and racial policing often increase during conflict. War gives cover to those who want to tighten control.

So Black people in Cherokee society navigated a battlefield on two levels:

- the battlefield of armies
- the battlefield of racial power

War and the Collapse of Everyday Life

Civil war destroys normal life. It breaks supply chains. It burns homes. It empties towns. It fractures families. It turns neighbors into informants. It forces the loyalty of oaths. It spreads disease and hunger.

In Indian Territory, these pressures were intensified by displacement on top of displacement. The Cherokee had already survived the removal. Now communities face another wave of disruption: raids, occupation, shifting control, and internal conflict.

War created refugees — Cherokee refugees, Black refugees, mixed families on the move, people fleeing violence, people searching for food and safety. Camps formed. Hunger spreads. Disease followed.

This is part of the story that rarely makes it into the citizenship debate, but it matters deeply: The Cherokee Freedmen's history is rooted in shared catastrophes. Black people in the Nation did not experience the war as outsiders watching the Cherokee suffering. They were inside it.

They suffered it too.
They survived it, too.

And their survival is part of the Nation's survival story, whether people want to admit it or not.

The Emancipation Question in Indian Territory

In the wider United States, emancipation came through a combination of policy and battlefield reality. In Indian Territory, emancipation was shaped by:

- military outcomes
- shifting federal policy
- and, most importantly, the post-war treaties the U.S. imposed on Native nations

For enslaved people in Cherokee society, the war raised a question that was both immediate and uncertain:

- If slavery ends, what happens to us here?
- Do we stay where our families are?
- Do we become citizens?
- Do we have land rights?
- Do we have political protection?
- Do we become targets?

For Cherokee leadership, emancipation raised a different set of questions:

- How much will the U.S. punish the Nation for wartime decisions?
- What will the U.S. demand in new treaties?
- Can sovereignty survive another round of federal restructuring?
- What happens to a social order where slavery has been part of economic life for some?

These questions would not be answered on a battlefield alone.

They would be answered on paper, through treaties.

And that is where the word "Freedman" begins to carry its most lasting power.

The War's Real Legacy: A Door Opens, and a Fight Begins

The Civil War ended slavery in law, but it did not automatically secure freedom in practice. For Cherokee

Freedmen, the end of the war opened a door. Yet, what waited on the other side was a new struggle: the fight to make freedom mean rights, belonging, and protection.

The war's legacy in Indian Territory was not only devastation. It was also a legal turning point. The U.S. used the post-war moment to reshape Native nations through treaty demands.

For the Cherokee Nation, the Treaty of 1866 would become a central document, one that promised citizenship to Freedmen and their descendants and tied that promise directly to the Nation's relationship with the United States.

***That promise is not ancient history.
It is a living history.***

And it is the backbone of modern debate.

In the next chapter, we turn to that treaty moment: the post-war negotiations, the 1866 Treaty's citizenship guarantee, and the beginning of a new era where rights would be promised in writing and then challenged for generations.

Because after the war, the question became clear:

If a treaty says someone belongs, who gets to overrule it: Cherokee tradition, Cherokee sovereignty, or the federal categories that were designed to divide us?

Chapter 9 - The 1866 Treaty: Citizenship Promised

The 1866 Treaty did not end the struggle.
It began the next one.

Because the moment citizenship was written into law, a new battle emerged: the battle over who would control the meaning of that citizenship. And in Indian Territory, that battle would be fought not only in council houses and courtrooms, but in homes, churches, neighborhoods, and the daily lives of Black Cherokees who were suddenly navigating a freedom that was both guaranteed and contested.

Freedom on Paper vs. Freedom in Practice

The treaty said Freedmen were citizens.
But citizenship on paper does not automatically translate into citizenship in daily life.

Freedmen still faced:

- hostility from some Cherokee citizens
- uncertainty about land rights
- attempts to limit political participation
- racial prejudice shaped by U.S. influence

- and the constant threat that the federal government might shift its position again

***Freedom is not a switch that flips.
It is a structure that must be built.***

And in the years after the treaty, Black Cherokees were building that structure while the ground beneath them kept shifting.

The Cherokee Nation's Reconstruction

Reconstruction in Indian Territory was not the same as Reconstruction in the South, but it carried similar tensions. The Cherokee Nation had to:

- rebuilding its government
- reestablish its courts
- redefine its political alliances
- and integrate Freedmen as citizens

This was not a small task.
It was re-founding.

And like any re-founding, it exposed every unresolved conflict inside the Nation.

Some Cherokee leaders honored the treaty fully.
Some resisted quietly.
Some resisted openly.
Some tried to reinterpret the treaty language to narrow its scope.
Some accepted Freedmen citizenship but wanted limits on land or political power.

And through all of this, Black Cherokees continued living, working, farming, worshiping, raising families, and participating in community life — because belonging is not something granted by paperwork. It is lived.

The Federal Government's Double Game

The United States had forced the treaty, but it did not enforce it consistently. Federal agents shifted positions depending on political winds, economic interests, and the broader agenda of Indian policy.

At times, the U.S. insisted that Freedmen must be treated as full citizens.

At other times, it looked the other way when Freedmen were excluded.

And when allotment approached, the federal government used the Freedmen category to divide the Nation even further.

This inconsistency was not accidental.
It was strategic.

A divided Cherokee Nation was easier to allot, easier to manage, and easier to reshape into the federal vision of "civilized" Indian communities.

The Treaty as a Living Document

For Freedmen and their descendants, the treaty became more than a legal text. It became:

- a shield
- a promise
- a historical anchor
- and a reminder that their belonging was not conditional

The treaty was the one place where the United States had written down, in clear language, that Black people in the Cherokee Nation were citizens — not guests, not dependents, not temporary residents, but citizens.

And that mattered.
It still matters.
Because when later generations tried to erase Freedmen from the Nation, the treaty stood as evidence that the erasure was not traditional. It was a revision.

The Seeds of the Next Era

The 1866 Treaty set the stage for everything that came next:

- the creation of the Dawes Commission
- the division of citizens into "by blood" and "Freedmen."
- the allotment of Cherokee land
- the federal push to dismantle tribal governments
- and the long-term weaponization of paperwork

The treaty was supposed to secure rights.
Instead, it became the starting point for a new kind of federal intrusion.

Because once the United States had a treaty that mentioned Freedmen, it used that treaty as justification to involve itself in Cherokee citizenship decisions for decades to come.

And once the U.S. created categories inside the Nation, it used those categories to reshape Cherokee identity into something measurable, sortable, and controllable.

Where the Story Goes from Here

The next chapter takes us into the era where the federal government perfected its administrative power: the roll-making period.

This is where:

- families were split
- identities were assigned

- blood quantum was invented as a tool
- and the categories "Cherokee by Blood" and "Cherokee Freedmen" were hardened into bureaucratic walls

This is the moment when federal paperwork began to override Cherokee memory, Cherokee kinship, and Cherokee tradition.

It is the moment when the United States created the divisions that modern debates still treat as if they were an ancient truth.

Because once identity is written down by an empire, the empire can claim it has always been that way.

And that is exactly what happened next.

Chapter 10 - Dawes Rolls: A Tool of Division

By the time the Dawes Commission arrived, the Cherokee Nation had already been counted, categorized, and recorded many times by the Nation itself and by the United States. The Dawes Rolls did not emerge as a fresh, objective effort to "get things right." They were layered on top of earlier rolls, censuses, and registries that were already flawed, inconsistent, and shaped by political goals rather than Cherokee reality.

Yet today, the Dawes Rolls are often treated as if they are the source of Cherokee identity.

They are not.

They are the moment when federal power hardened earlier confusion into permanent division.

Rolls Before Dawes: A Shaky Foundation

Long before the Dawes Commission, multiple rolls existed for different purposes: treaty compliance, annuity distribution, removal logistics, population counts, and political control. These rolls were never designed to define Cherokee citizenship forever. They were tools for specific moments, created under pressure, often by outsiders unfamiliar with Cherokee language, kinship, or community structure.

Across these earlier rolls, problems were common:

- names misspelled, translated inconsistently, or replaced with English names, breaking family continuity on paper
- Cherokee speakers misunderstood or mis-recorded by English-speaking officials
- families appearing differently from roll to roll, depending on who collected the information and why
- race applied unevenly, sometimes ignored, sometimes emphasized — based on shifting political needs
- people moving, communities reorganizing, and records lagging lived reality

These inconsistencies mattered, but they were not always fatal because no single roll yet claimed final authority over identity.

That changed with Dawes.

Why the Dawes Commission Existed

The Dawes Rolls were created for one overriding purpose: to break tribal landownership.

The United States wanted to dismantle communal landholding in Indian Territory and open so-called "surplus" land to non-Native settlement. Allotment required individual ownership. Individual ownership required a list of individuals. And that list required the federal government to decide who counted.

The Dawes Commission was not a cultural project.
It was a land project.

Enrollment under Dawes was not about honoring Cherokee belonging. It was about determining who would receive land allotments and how much land could be declared excess and taken.

Once identity became tied to land distribution, enrollment became power.

From Record to Authority

***Earlier rolls documented people.
Dawes defined them.***

The Dawes process shifted Cherokee identity away from community recognition and toward federal authority. It treated citizenship as something to be proven to outsiders, rather than affirmed within Cherokee society.

This created immediate danger:

- people who belonged could be excluded
- political influence could shape outcomes
- Errors could be locked in permanently
- categories could override family and kinship

Most damaging of all, Dawes did not resolve contradictions between earlier rolls. It simply selected a classification and made it final.

"By Blood" and "Freedmen": Manufacturing Separation

The Dawes Commission divided Cherokee citizens into rigid tracks:

- Cherokee by Blood
- Cherokee Freedmen

These categories were not traditional. They were not rooted in Cherokee law or kinship. They were administrative shortcuts designed to make the allotment easier.

Race became the dominant sorting mechanism. If a person was Black, they were likely placed on the Freedmen roll even if they had Cherokee ancestry, Cherokee family ties, or prior recognition on earlier rolls.

This is not speculation.
Some individuals listed as Freedmen on the Dawes Rolls were listed as Cherokee by blood on earlier rolls.

That single fact exposes the myth of Dawes' accuracy.

Identity did not change.
Paper did.

Families Divided on Paper

One of the most devastating consequences of Dawes was the splitting of families by category.

Parents and children could be assigned different statuses.
Siblings could be separated administratively.
Cherokee ancestry could disappear from a family's legal identity in a single generation — not because it was untrue, but because it was inconvenient to federal racial logic.

In a kinship-based society, family defines belonging.
Under Dawes, the file replaced the family.

And once the file became authoritative, the damage did not stop with one generation.

Errors That Became Inheritance

The Dawes Rolls contain mistakes — clerical errors, racial assumptions, rushed decisions, and contradictions with earlier records. But unlike earlier rolls, Dawes' errors became permanent.

If your ancestor was misclassified, that classification followed your descendants.

If Cherokee ancestry was erased at Dawes, blood-quantum calculations treated it as if it never existed at all.

Blood quantum did not correct errors.
It amplified them.

By turning identity into fractions based on flawed records, the system ensured that mistakes would compound over time, shrinking recognition while pretending to apply objective math.

This was not accidental.

Blood quantum is a federal invention designed to reduce the number of people legally recognized as Native over generations. When combined with Dawes-era misclassification, it became an erasure engine.

Why the Freedmen Category Was So Useful

The Freedmen designation did more than separate people; it stabilized division.

By creating a permanent administrative category tied to race, the U.S. ensured:

- a divided citizenry
- weakened political unity
- easier land dispossession
- future justifications for exclusion

A fully united Cherokee Nation, fully including Freedmen descendants as equal citizens under the treaty promise, would have been harder to dismantle. The division made federal management easier.

That is the colonial pattern: divide, categorize, control.

The Roll as a Modern Weapon

Today, the Dawes Rolls are often treated as sacred proof of who is "really" Cherokee. But the Rolls were created after Cherokee citizenship already existed, after earlier rolls already conflicted, and after the 1866 Treaty already promised citizenship to Freedmen and their descendants.

Using Dawes categories to deny citizenship relies on circular logic:

- A dividing system creates separation
- The separation is treated as evidence of natural difference
- The evidence is then used to justify continued exclusion

The wall is built and then cited as proof that people were never meant to be together.

What This Chapter Makes Clear

Taken together, the full roll history shows:

- The Dawes Rolls were not the first rolls
- earlier rolls already contained inconsistencies and errors
- Dawes did not correct those problems; it froze them
- Some Dawes Freedmen were listed as Cherokee by blood on earlier rolls
- Race, not kinship, drove Dawes's classification
- blood quantum magnified misclassification into generational erasure

- Modern reliance on Dawes repeats a federal project of division

Records matter, but they are not sacred. They must be read critically, in context, and with an understanding of who created them and why.

When colonial paperwork is treated as truth without question, living people pay the price.

Where We Go Next

In the next chapter, we move from paper to consequence, examining how these classifications affected land ownership, political voice, and everyday life for Freedmen families as Oklahoma statehood and Jim Crow hardened racial boundaries even further.

Because once bureaucracy replaces kinship, injustice no longer needs chains.

Chapter 11 - When Paper Overruled Kinship

The shift from kinship to paperwork didn't just change how the Cherokee Nation functioned. It changed how people saw themselves — and how they were seen. Once the federal government succeeded in making paper the arbiter of identity, the consequences rippled outward into every corner of Cherokee life.

And those consequences did not fall evenly.

They fell hardest on the people the United States had already marked as targets: Black people.
Black Cherokees.
Freedmen descendants.
Families whose belonging had been lived for generations, but whose identities could now be erased with a pen.

The Rise of a Two-Tiered Cherokee Society

The Dawes categories created a two-tiered system within the Nation:

- **Cherokee by Blood** were treated as the "real" Cherokees
- **Cherokee Freedmen** were treated as conditional, peripheral, or lesser

This was not a Cherokee tradition.

This was the American racial hierarchy imported into Cherokee governance.

And once the categories existed, people began to internalize them.
Not everyone. Not everywhere. But enough.

Enough that:

- Freedmen families were questioned more often
- their claims to ancestry were doubted
- their political participation was scrutinized
- their land was more vulnerable
- their children were treated differently in schools and churches
- their presence was framed as something to be justified rather than assumed

This is how colonial systems work:
They don't just impose categories. They teach people to believe in them.

The Social Weight of a Federal Label

A federal label is not just a label.
It becomes a lens.

Once someone is labeled "Freedman," people begin to see them through that category:

- not as a neighbor
- not as a relative
- not as a Cherokee
- but as a bureaucratic classification

And because the category was racialized, it carried all the weight of American anti-Blackness with it.

This meant that even when Freedmen descendants lived fully inside Cherokee culture, speaking the language, participating in ceremonies, attending Cherokee churches, and living in Cherokee communities, the label could still be used to push them to the margins.

The label became a wall.
A wall built by the United States.
A wall maintained by bureaucracy.
A wall that some people began to mistake for tradition.

The Emotional Toll of Being Treated as a Footnote

For many Black Cherokee families, the roll era created a generational wound, a wound that did not come from physical violence, but from erasure.

Erasure is its own kind of violence.

It looks like:

- being told your ancestors don't count
- being told your family stories are lies
- being told your identity is "political."
- being told your belonging is conditional
- being told your history is secondary
- being told your presence is an inconvenience

It looks like being asked to prove what others are allowed to assume.

It looks like watching people with less historical connection to Cherokee life claim more legitimacy because their paperwork fits the federal mold.

It looks like it's being treated as if your ancestors were only ever laborers, never kin.

This is the psychological cost of colonial paperwork, a cost that rarely appears in official histories, but lives in the memories and bodies of the people who endured it.

The Slow Drift Toward Exclusion

Once paper overruled kinship, exclusion became easier.

Not immediately.
Not total.
But easier.

It began with:

- questioning Freedmen land claims
- limiting political participation
- treating Freedmen rolls as separate and lesser
- using blood quantum to shrink recognition
- framing Freedmen descendants as "not really Cherokee."

And over time, these patterns hardened into policy.

The tragedy is that many people came to believe these policies reflected Cherokee tradition when they reflected federal engineering.

Colonial systems are most successful when they convince the colonized that the colonizer's categories are their own.

The Intergenerational Impact

The consequences of the roll era did not end with the people who lived through it. They shaped the lives of their children, grandchildren, and great-grandchildren.

Freedmen descendants inherited:

- land loss

- political exclusion
- social suspicion
- racial stigma
- bureaucratic barriers
- the burden of proof

Meanwhile, the descendants of those classified "by blood" inherited:

- political advantage
- social legitimacy
- easier access to resources
- unquestioned belonging

This is not about blame.
It is about structure.

Structures create outcomes.
And the structure that Dawes created was designed to divide.

Why This History Still Matters

Some people ask why this history still matters today.
Why revisit the pain?
Why reopen old wounds?

Because the wounds were never allowed to heal.

Because the categories created during the roll era are still used today in citizenship debates, in political arguments, in community conversations, in the quiet judgments people make about who "looks Cherokee" and who doesn't.

Because the paperwork that overruled kinship is still treated as a sacred truth.

Because the descendants of those misclassified are still fighting for recognition, their ancestors already lived.

Because the treaty promise of 1866 is still being debated as if it were optional.

Because the story of Black Cherokees is still being pushed to the margins of Cherokee history, even though it is central to the Nation's survival story.

Where This Leads

The next chapter takes us into the moment when all these forces, Dawes, allotment, racial hierarchy, misclassification, and federal intrusion collided with a new political reality:

Oklahoma Statehood.

Statehood brought Jim Crow.
Jim Crow brought segregation.
Segregation brought new forms of exclusion and violence.

And Black Cherokee families already navigating the harm of the roll-era division were forced into an even tighter cage.

Because once Indian Territory became Oklahoma, the racial rules of the American South did not stay at the border.

They became law.

Chapter 12 - Oklahoma Statehood and Further Marginalization

When Indian Territory became the state of Oklahoma, it wasn't just a name change. It was a change of rules, and for Black people, those rules were already written in the language of segregation.

Statehood meant the political and legal systems surrounding the Cherokee Nation hardened into something more permanent: a state government empowered to enforce racial hierarchy, and a broader American society entering one of the most aggressive eras of Jim Crow. That shift didn't stay outside the Cherokee communities. It pressed in, shaped daily life, and intensified the damage already done by roll-era divisions.

For Cherokee Freedmen descendants and Black Cherokees, Oklahoma statehood created a double bind:

- Federal policy had already sorted them into a separate category on paper.
- Now state society sorted them into a separate caste in public life.

The result was further marginalization. Not because Black Cherokee families were absent from Cherokee life, but because law and custom were engineered to push them to the edges.

Statehood: A New Government Sitting on Old Dispossession

Oklahoma's formation was made possible by the dismantling of tribal land systems. Allotment had already fractured communal landholding. "Surplus" land had already been opened to non-Native settlement. Tribal governance has already weakened through federal control.

So, when statehood arrived, it didn't come into a neutral space. It arrived on top of a landscape reshaped by dispossession.

For many Native nations, statehood represented another step in a long project: turning sovereign peoples into minorities inside a state system designed without them in mind.

For Black Cherokee families, the danger was magnified. Oklahoma was not just a state. It was a state entering the American racial order at a time when that order was hardening violently.

Jim Crow Didn't Ask Permission

Segregation was not simply a social custom. It was law backed by force.

In the Jim Crow era, Black people were pushed into separate schools, separate public facilities, separate neighborhoods, and separate political realities. Voting power was attacked. Economic independence was targeted. Violence and intimidation enforced boundaries when paperwork did not.

Black Cherokee families lived inside this system, whether they wanted to or not.

And here is the key point: even though Cherokee history is distinct from white Southern history, the state's racial system did not care about that distinction. Jim Crow did not ask whether you were Cherokee. It asked where you fit in America's racial hierarchy.

So Black Cherokees and Freedmen descendants faced pressure from the outside that was relentless:

- racial classification in state records
- segregation in schools and public life
- policing that treated Blackness as criminal
- economic limits placed on Black communities
- the threat of racial violence

At the same time, inside Cherokee political life, roll-era categories could be used to question belonging.

Outside and inside pressures reinforced each other.

Schools: Where Segregation Shaped Identity

Education is one of the quiet places where history becomes permanent.

Segregated schooling did more than separate children. It shaped who was considered part of which community, who learned which histories, who had access to which opportunities, and who grew up with a sense of belonging versus a sense of being tolerated.

In Oklahoma, where Black communities worked hard to build their own schools and institutions in the face of exclusion, education became both a site of harm and a site of strength. Black Cherokee families often had to rely on Black institutions for safety and opportunity because the broader system did not offer them protection.

But there was a cost: segregation forced a separation in daily life that could later be misread as "separate identity," when it was imposed separation.

A person can be Cherokee and still be forced into "colored" spaces by the state.

That contradiction became a lived reality for generations.

Land and Wealth: The Targeting of Black Ownership

Statehood also intensified economic vulnerability.

Allotment had already placed individual landowners into a system where property could be lost through fraud, debt, manipulation, and legal pressure. For Black landowners, those vulnerabilities were often sharper because the wider society treated Black land as something that should not exist.

Black prosperity has historically been treated as a threat in America. When Black people accumulate land, business, or political power, systems tend to form around the question: How do we take it?

That question hovered over Black communities in Oklahoma, and Black Cherokee communities were not immune. Even when families held land, keeping it across generations was a battle against:

- predatory contracts
- legal systems that favored wealth and whiteness
- intimidation
- violence or the threat of it
- bureaucratic traps that turned technicalities into dispossession

This is one of the reasons modern identity debates can feel disconnected from economic reality. People argue about belonging as if it were purely symbolic, while ignoring the fact that these systems of classification were tied directly to land and resources.

Citizenship on Paper vs. Citizenship in Practice

Here is the harsh truth: legal recognition does not guarantee lived equality.

Even when Cherokee Freedmen descendants had treaty-backed citizenship rights, their day-to-day experience could still reflect a different reality, especially in a state society built on segregation.

This produced a painful tension:

- Cherokee identity rooted in kinship and community
- federal roll categories that separated Freedmen from "by blood" citizens
- state Jim Crow laws that treated Blackness as a permanent second-class status

In practice, many Black Cherokee families were asked to navigate overlapping exclusions:

- excluded from white spaces by Jim Crow
- questioned in Cherokee spaces by roll-era stigma
- forced to prove identity in ways others were not asked to prove

That is not simply "discrimination."
It is layered marginalization designed to exhaust people until they stop fighting.

Survival and Institution-Building

And yet Black Cherokee families survived.

Not by waiting for permission.

They survived through community building: churches, schools, mutual aid, family networks, and businesses. They survived through adaptation: knowing when to keep your head down and when to stand your ground. They survived through memory: keeping family stories alive even when official narratives tried to erase them. They survived through leadership: elders, organizers, educators, and everyday people who refused to let their children grow up believing they were nobody.

This matters because survival itself becomes evidence. When people argue today as if Freedmen descendants "weren't part of Cherokee life," they ignore the reality that Black Cherokee families have been building, working, worshiping, and contributing in Oklahoma since before statehood and long after it.

Erasure is not proof of absence.
It is proof of power.

How Oklahoma's Racial Order Influenced Tribal Debates

Another uncomfortable truth: state society influences tribal society.

Oklahoma's Jim Crow culture did not stay neatly outside Native governance. It shaped attitudes, politics, and definitions of legitimacy. It encouraged racial thinking that aligned with the broader American hierarchy, which treated Blackness as separation rather than kinship.

Over time, this helped harden the idea that "Freedmen" and "Cherokee" were separate categories of people, even when history and family ties contradicted that separation.

This is how colonization evolves: it doesn't only take land.
It changes what people believe about themselves and each other.

What This Chapter Establishes

By the end of this chapter, the reader should understand:

- Oklahoma statehood intensified the marginalization created by roll-era classifications.
- Jim Crow racial laws treated Blackness as a caste regardless of Cherokee ties.
- Segregation shaped education, opportunity, and public life for Black Cherokee families.
- Land ownership became even more vulnerable under state systems and racial targeting.
- Citizenship rights on paper did not guarantee equal life in practice.
- Black Cherokee survival continued through community institutions and memory.
- State racial ideology influenced how tribal debates about belonging later hardened.

In the next chapter, we move deeper into the 20th century — how Cherokee Nation governance rebuilt, how sovereignty was reasserted, and how the question of Freedmen citizenship remained unresolved beneath the surface, waiting to re-emerge in modern legal and political conflict.

Because history does not disappear when it isn't talked about.
It waits.

Chapter 13 - Cherokee Nation in the 20th Century

The 20th century is often told as a story of Native disappearance — tribes fading into the background of American life, reduced to stereotypes or treated like relics. But the Cherokee Nation did not disappear. It endured. It adapted. It carried culture through periods designed to smother it. It rebuilt political life in the face of federal interference. And it entered modern times still wrestling with the same unresolved tension that runs through this entire book:

Who gets to define belonging, Cherokee people, or colonial systems built to divide us?

For Cherokee Freedmen descendants and Black Cherokees, the 20th century carried another painful layer. Even as the Nation survived and strengthened, roll-era categories and Jim Crow racial logic continued to shape who was seen as "real," who was centered, and who was treated as an asterisk.

This chapter traces how Cherokee governance and identity moved through the 20th century, how sovereignty was reshaped, how community survived, and how the Freedmen question remained present even when it was pushed out of public conversation.

Survival Under Federal Control

In the early 1900s, tribal sovereignty across Indian Country was under heavy federal restriction. U.S. policies had already dismantled communal landholding and pushed Native governance into a position where federal oversight could limit political power.

For Cherokee citizens, this period created a contradiction:

- Cherokee people continued to exist as a nation culturally and socially.
- But federal policy narrowed the Nation's political space.

This is one of the most important patterns in Cherokee history: the U.S. repeatedly tried to reduce Native nations to cultural artifacts without political power.

But the Cherokee Nation remained a living community. Families continued. Churches continued. Ceremonies continued. Language persisted sometimes openly, sometimes quietly, sometimes in fragments held by elders and passed on in private.

And throughout these decades, Cherokee identity was not determined solely by federal paperwork in everyday life. Communities still knew who their people were. Kinship still mattered. But the official authority of rolls and federal categories continued to shape access, recognition, and rights.

That mattered profoundly for Freedmen descendants.

The Roll Categories Didn't Disappear — They Settled In

One of the most deceptive things about roll-era classification is that it becomes invisible over time. People grow up inheriting the categories as if they were natural.

"Cherokee by Blood."
"Freedmen."

As if these were ancient, sacred divisions.

But as we've established, those categories were federal administrative tools built on earlier inconsistent rolls, hardened by Dawes, and influenced by American racial hierarchy. Even when the Nation moved through new eras, those categories remained embedded in how identity was argued, challenged, and sometimes policed.

For Freedmen descendants, the lived impact often looked like this:

- being Cherokee in daily life, but questioned in formal contexts
- carrying Cherokee family history, but treated as if paper overruled that history
- watching Cherokee institutions grow stronger while still feeling like membership was conditional

This created a generational strain, one that rarely makes it into official histories because official histories prefer a clean narrative of tribal revival.

But revival with unresolved exclusion is not complete revival.

Identity as Culture vs. Identity as Gatekeeping

Across the 20th century, Cherokee identity continued to be lived through cultural family networks, place, language, and community responsibility. Yet at the same time, American society pushed identity toward gatekeeping, who could access resources, who could claim benefits, and who could be counted.

This tension grew sharper as federal programs tied "Indian" identity to documentation and eligibility. The more resources were connected to proof, the more proof became contested.

And when proof becomes contested, people begin to treat identity like property.

The question stops being "Who are your people?"
and becomes "What do you have that proves it?"

This shift is not a Cherokee tradition. It is the logic of bureaucracy and scarcity.

And it landed hard on Freedmen descendants, because their documentation was already shaped by a category designed to separate them.

Black Cherokee Life in the Mid-Century

The mid-20th century was a period of contradictions for Black Cherokee families.

On one side, Black communities in Oklahoma, like Black communities across America, built strength through churches, schools, businesses, and organizing. They survived segregation by creating parallel institutions that protected dignity and community life.

On the other side, segregation also forced separations that outsiders later misinterpreted as natural. Black Cherokee families might live, worship, and educate their children in Black spaces because white spaces were violent and exclusionary. Not because they were separate from Cherokee history.

This matters because identity debates often ignore the reality of survival under Jim Crow. They interpret imposed separation as evidence of "difference," rather than evidence of racist structure.

Meanwhile, Cherokee communities continued their own survival in a state that often treated Native people as obstacles or curiosities. So, both Native and Black communities were forced to navigate Oklahoma's racial hierarchy sometimes in parallel, sometimes intertwined, sometimes in conflict, often under pressure from the same systems.

Black Cherokee families lived in that intersection.

And intersections are always where the hardest truths sit.

The Quiet Continuity of Treaty Rights

Even when the Freedmen citizenship question wasn't dominating headlines, the treaty promises still existed.

Treaty rights don't vanish because people stop talking about them.
But enforcement weakens when memory is attacked.

Across the 20th century, Freedmen descendants often experienced a slow drift: treaty citizenship recognized in principle but increasingly challenged in practice, especially as roll categories hardened and political narratives changed.

This is the danger of time:

- A promise can be legally intact
- and socially undermined

- until the next generation grows up believing the undermining was always true

When that happens, a treaty begins to feel like an argument rather than an obligation.

That is not just a historical drift.
That is political engineering.

Rebuilding Government and Modern Cherokee Nationhood

By the late 20th century, the Cherokee Nation's governance and institutional presence strengthened. The Nation expanded services, increased political organization, and built modern structures that made Cherokee sovereignty more visible and durable.

This period is often celebrated, and it should be. The survival and rebuilding of Cherokee governance after everything the United States attempted is not a small achievement. It is a national endurance.

But rebuilding also raised a question that comes up every time a nation grows stronger:

Who is included in the "we"?

A growing government administers membership. It manages resources. It defines access. It issues documentation. And when documentation becomes central, old roll categories return with new force.

For Freedmen descendants, this era could feel like watching a Nation rise while still standing outside the full embrace of that rise — even when their families had never left.

This is not a matter of "hurt feelings."
It is a matter of political belonging.

The Ground Beneath the Modern Conflict

The modern citizenship battles did not appear out of nowhere. They were built on decades of unresolved tension:

- roll categories treated as identity truth
- treaty promises treated as optional history
- Jim Crow racial logic lingering in social attitudes
- federal paperwork becoming central to eligibility
- identity becoming politicized through scarcity and power

By the end of the 20th century, the stage was set.

All the elements were present:

- a treaty promise of Freedmen citizenship
- a bureaucratic system that separated Freedmen from "by blood."
- a political environment where sovereignty was being reasserted
- and a racialized American context that still treated Black belonging as suspicious

What was missing was a trigger, something that would force the question back into the open.

That trigger would come.

What This Chapter Establishes

By the end of this chapter, the reader should understand:

- The Cherokee Nation survived and rebuilt through the 20th century despite federal restrictions.
- Roll-era categories remained embedded and continued shaping perceptions of legitimacy.

- Identity tensions grew as documentation became tied to eligibility and resources.

- Black Cherokee families lived at the intersection of Cherokee survival and Jim Crow racial order.

- Treaty rights did not disappear — but memory and enforcement were weakened over time.

- Modern Cherokee governance strengthened, raising renewed debates about who is included.

- The modern citizenship conflict was not sudden. It was the result of long-standing pressures.

In the next chapter, we step into the modern era where conflict becomes unavoidable: citizenship battles, disenrollment efforts, and court decisions that forced the Nation, the federal government, and the public to confront what the 1866 Treaty promised and whether those promises still mean anything.

***Because a nation can't outrun its obligations.
Not forever.***

Chapter 14 - Citizenship Battles and Courtrooms

At some point, history stops being something you study and becomes something you live on.

For Cherokee Freedmen descendants, that moment arrived repeatedly in the modern era — when citizenship was treated not as a shared bond of nationhood, but as a contested prize. When the meaning of "Cherokee" was argued like a property line. When families who had lived Cherokee life for generations were told, directly or indirectly, that their belonging was up for debate.

And when paper once again was given more authority than kinship.

This chapter is not just about lawsuits and legislation. It is about power: who holds it, how it is used, and how colonial categories can be revived inside Native governance even after the Nation has fought so hard to survive colonization.

The modern conflict over Cherokee Freedmen citizenship is often framed as a clash between sovereignty and civil rights. But that framing hides a deeper reality: the 1866 Treaty is not a civil-rights suggestion. It is a nation-to-nation obligation. And the conflict is not whether the Cherokee Nation has sovereignty

— it does. The conflict is how sovereignty is practiced, and whether it aligns with Cherokee values and treaty commitments.

How the Question Returned

For many years, Freedmen citizenship simmered beneath the surface — present in family stories, in community life, in quiet exclusions, and in the weight of Dawes-era categories. But modern Cherokee Nation governance also grew stronger, expanded services, and increased the significance of official citizenship status.

When citizenship becomes the gateway to healthcare, housing support, educational programs, and political participation, the stakes rise. Not because those benefits are "handouts," but because they are expressions of nationhood, tangible ways a Nation cares for its citizens.

As the Nation's capacity grew, so did the intensity around the question:

Who is a citizen?

And in that moment, the Dawes-era divisions, "by blood" vs. "Freedmen", were pulled out of the archive and treated like moral truth rather than what they were: administrative tools built during allotment.

That is when the debate shifted from historical tension to open political conflict.

Disenrollment: When a Nation Removes Its Own People

Disenrollment is one of the most painful acts a nation can commit against its own citizens. It is not simply "updating records." It is the removal of belonging. It changes a person's legal identity, their political voice, and their relationship to their Nation.

In Cherokee Freedmen's history, disenrollment efforts, whether fully enacted or threatened, were experienced as a kind of second removal.

Not removal from land,
but removal from citizenship.

And because the Freedmen category was racialized, the threat carried an additional message: that Blackness itself could be treated as a reason to question Cherokee belonging.

To those living in this reality, it did not feel like an abstract constitutional debate. It felt like being told your Nation was willing to cut you loose.

The Legal Battlefield: Treaty Logic vs. Roll Logic

In modern disputes, two competing frameworks collide:

1. Treaty Logic
The 1866 Treaty promised citizenship to Freedmen and their descendants. Under treaty logic, the question is straightforward:

The treaty guarantees citizenship, so Freedmen descendants are citizens.

2. Roll Logic
Roll logic treats Dawes categories as the primary foundation of citizenship, especially "Cherokee by Blood." Under this framework, the argument becomes:

If your ancestor was on the Freedmen roll, you are not Cherokee "by blood," therefore, citizenship can be denied.

The problem is that roll logic treats a federal administrative system — known to contain inconsistencies, contradictions, and race-based misclassification as if it overrides treaty obligations.

In other words, it allows a later colonial tool to undermine an earlier nation-to-nation promise.

That is not history.
That is a political choice.

And it repeats the original colonial strategy: divide the Nation by paper and then treat paper as destiny.

Sovereignty and the Temptation of Simplification

Sovereignty is real. Cherokee Nation sovereignty is not a gift from the United States; it is inherent. But sovereignty also comes with responsibility: to law, to values, to the people, and to the Nation's own commitments.

In modern debates, "sovereignty" is sometimes used like a shield to stop conversation:

"We can decide citizenship however we want."

But sovereignty is not strong when it ignores obligations.
It is strongest when it honors them.

A nation that demands treaty recognition for land and jurisdiction must also respect treaty commitments that define citizenship. You cannot argue that treaties are sacred when they protect Native power and irrelevant when they protect Freedmen citizens.

Selective treaty respect turns sovereignty into convenience.

And convenience is not a national principle.

Courts: Where Cherokee Identity Was Put on Trial

When the conflict moved into courts, it forced the issue into a setting that is always uncomfortable for Native nations: American legal systems.

Cherokee people have long understood that U.S. courts can be hostile, inconsistent, and shaped by political winds. But the tragedy here is that Freedmen descendants often had to go to court not to attack sovereignty, but to force recognition of rights already promised.

That is an ugly position to be placed in:

- A Native citizen seeking recognition within their Nation
- Forced to appeal through systems that have historically harmed Native nations
- Because internal politics were treating an administrative category as a reason to deny treaty citizenship

This is how colonial pressure shows up again: it forces Native communities into conflict and then watches from the outside.

Still, the court arena produced something important: it required claims to be measured against treaty language and legal history, not just political rhetoric.

In that setting, the reality of the 1866 Treaty could not be waved away as "opinion."

It had to be confronted.

The Human Reality Behind the Legal War

While lawyers argued, families lived.

Children watched their parents fight for recognition. Elders watched the Nation debate whether their grandchildren belonged. People who had spent their lives identifying as Cherokee — through community ties, family history, cultural practice — were told they were "really" something else because of a line on a roll created during allotment.

This is what bureaucratic identity does: it turns a living person into a category debate.

And it produces a very specific kind of harm:

- anxiety about belonging
- distrust inside communities
- fear of losing services
- shame planted where pride should be
- a generational wound that tells people they are conditional citizens

Even when a person wins a legal argument, the social scar remains.

The Deeper Truth: This Was Never Only About Paper

Modern citizenship battles are often presented as technical disputes:

- What the Constitution says
- What the rolls show
- What category applies
- What eligibility rules should be

But underneath that technical language is the deeper reality:

This conflict is about whether Cherokee identity will be defined through a racialized colonial framework or through Cherokee integrity and treaty responsibility.

Because once "Freedmen" is treated as a permanent separation, rather than a legal status born from emancipation, Blackness becomes an implied disqualifier.

And that is not a Cherokee value.
That is an American racial value.

What This Chapter Establishes

By the end of this chapter, the reader should understand:

- The modern Freedmen conflict reemerged as Cherokee governance grew and citizenship gained higher stakes.
- Disenrollment and exclusion efforts functioned as a modern form of removal for Freedmen descendants.
- The central legal conflict is treaty logic vs. roll logic.
- Dawes-era categories are being treated as permanent truth despite documented inconsistencies and misclassification.
- *Sovereignty is not weakened by honoring treaty obligations. It is strengthened.*
- Court battles forced the treaty's promise back into public view.
- The human cost of these disputes is generational and deeply personal.

In the next chapter, we step out of the courtroom and back into the heart of the book's message: what it means to say, ***"We are Cherokee"***, not as a slogan, but as a statement of lived identity, historical truth, and national integrity.

Because if Cherokee history is honest, then Cherokee future must be honest too.

Chapter 15 - We Are Cherokee

Some people hear the words *"We are Cherokee"* and immediately ask for proof.

Not because they want to understand, but because they want a gate, a way to stand at the entrance of the Nation and decide who gets to pass. For Cherokee Freedmen descendants, that demand for proof has become a familiar ritual. One that is rarely applied equally and seldom applied with the same suspicion to everyone.

But Cherokee identity is not a courtroom performance.
It is not a category that begins and ends on a federal roll.
And it is not a fear.

Cherokee identity is a living relationship between people, land, language, memory, responsibility, and community. That relationship existed before the United States counted us. It survived when the United States tried to remove us. And it persists even when colonial paperwork is treated as sacred.

This chapter is about reclaiming the center of the conversation: not what the Dawes Commission wrote down, but what Cherokee life has been.

Identity Is Lived, Not Assigned

The most honest way to understand Cherokee belonging is to look at how it was practiced before it was bureaucratized.

Cherokee citizenship was historically tied to kinship, clan, community recognition, and responsibility. It was tied to how you lived among the people. That is why the traditional meaning of "Fullblood" matters so much in this conversation: it was never originally about math or fractions. It was about living fully in Cherokee ways — language, customs, responsibilities, values.

When you start from that foundation, you realize something that roll-based arguments try to avoid:

There is no traditional Cherokee principle that says Blackness cancels Cherokee belonging.

That idea comes from the American racial hierarchy, not Cherokee kinship.

So, when Freedmen descendants say, "We are Cherokee," they are not inventing a new identity. They are naming a reality formed through Cherokee history through removal, through war, through rebuilding, through shared life in Tahlequah, and across Cherokee communities.

Black Cherokee Life Is Not a Footnote

One of the most harmful habits in this debate is treating Black Cherokee history as an "issue" rather than as part of the Nation's story.

Black people in Cherokee society did not appear only at emancipation. They were present before removal. They were forced west on the Trail of Tears. They lived and labored in Cherokee households and communities. Some were enslaved. Some were free. Many formed families and communities that endured long after slavery ended.

The label "Freedman" was a federal term created to describe emancipation. It was not a Cherokee invention, and it was never meant to become a permanent identity wall. Yet over time, it was used that way. Especially once the Dawes Rolls separated citizens into categories, and later generations treated those categories as if they were sacred.

But the lived reality is older than the label.

Black Cherokee families have been part of Cherokee life in Oklahoma for generations. Their existence is not a modern argument. It is a historical fact.

Sovereignty With Integrity

In modern debate, sovereignty is often spoken of as if it were only about power. The power to decide. But sovereignty is also about responsibility. The responsibility to honor the Nation's commitments, to practice justice according to Cherokee values, and to refuse colonial frameworks designed to divide us.

The 1866 Treaty is not a rumor. It is not a moral suggestion. It is a nation-to-nation agreement promising citizenship to Freedmen and their descendants.

If Cherokee sovereignty depends on the United States honoring treaties, then Cherokee sovereignty must also honor treaty obligations within the Nation. Otherwise, sovereignty becomes selectively strong when it benefits us, flexible when it requires sacrifice.

Integrity means we do not treat treaty rights like a buffet.
Integrity means we do not use federal paperwork created for allotment as if it outweighs treaty promises and community reality.

Integrity means we do not allow the Dawes Commission to define Cherokee identity more than the Cherokee people do.

The Damage of Exclusion Is National Damage

When Freedmen descendants are excluded or treated as conditional citizens, the harm is not limited to those families alone.

Exclusion damages the Cherokee Nation itself.

It teaches Cherokee people to trust colonial categories over Cherokee history. It reinforces racial thinking that comes from outside our traditions. It creates internal divisions that weaken political unity. It turns citizens into adversaries. It replaces shared responsibility with suspicion.

And it tells the world that the Cherokee Nation can be pressured into adopting the same racial hierarchies that were used to justify slavery and dispossession in the first place.

That is not strength.
That is colonial success.

A Nation does not become safer by shrinking its truth.
It becomes smaller.

"Belonging" Is a Cherokee Value

One of the most overlooked truths in all of this is that traditional Cherokee values are not built around fear of contamination. They are built around relationships, responsibility, and balance.

Cherokee society understood adoption, incorporation, alliance, and kinship as part of national survival. That does not mean identity is meaningless. It means identity is relational and lived.

So, when we speak about Freedmen descendants, the question should not be framed as:

113

"How do we protect ourselves from them?"

It should be framed as:

"What does it mean to honor our history, our promises, and our people?"

Because Freedmen descendants are not strangers asking to be invited into Cherokee history.
They are already in the story.

Reconciliation Without Erasure

Reconciliation is not pretending slavery didn't happen. It is not pretending that the Dawes Rolls didn't divide people. It is not pretending pain doesn't exist.

Reconciliation is truth-telling paired with action.

It requires the Cherokee Nation to face its full history — slavery, war, treaty promises, roll-era division, and modern political conflict — without reducing any of it to propaganda.

It also requires Cherokee citizens to reject the temptation to treat Black Cherokee identity as a threat. The threat has never been the presence of Freedmen descendants. The threat has been the colonial system that trained everyone to believe division is natural.

Healing requires refusing that training.

It requires saying, clearly:
We will not let colonial categories become Cherokee law in our hearts.

The Future Is a Choice

History created this conflict, but the future will be decided by choice.

The Cherokee Nation can choose to define itself through:

- treaty responsibility
- kinship-centered belonging
- historical truth
- sovereignty practiced with integrity

Or it can choose to define itself through:

- federal roll categories created for allotment
- racial logic inherited from Jim Crow
- a shrinking idea of belonging that treats identity as a defensive wall

One path strengthens the Nation by aligning with truth.
The other path strengthens colonial narratives by repeating them.

And in the end, the Nation will be remembered not only by what it survived, but by what it chose to become.
What This Chapter Says, Plainly

This is what "We are Cherokee" means in this book:

- *We are Cherokee because our families lived in Cherokee history.*
- *We are Cherokee because belonging predates the rolls.*
- *We are Cherokee because treaties promised citizenship, and those promises still matter.*
- *We are Cherokee because Black Cherokee life is part of Cherokee life.*

- *We are Cherokee because identity is not erased by a category created for allotment.*
- *We are Cherokee because sovereignty without integrity is not the sovereignty our ancestors fought for.*

The words are not a plea.
They are a statement.

Closing Into the Conclusion

In the conclusion, we will step back and speak directly to the Nation's future. What it means to practice sovereignty with responsibility, how truth strengthens identity rather than diluting it, and why honoring Freedmen citizenship is not surrendering Cherokee Nationhood but affirming it.

Because a Nation does not lose itself by telling the truth.
It loses itself by refusing to tell the truth.

CONCLUSION - Honoring the Whole Truth

I wrote this book because I'm a Black Cherokee from Tahlequah — because I've lived in Cherokee stories my whole life, and I've watched which stories get carried out front like a flag... and which ones get tucked away like they're dangerous.

Cherokee Freedmen's history has been treated as if it is dangerous. Not because it's false, but because it's true. And because truth has a way of forcing choices.

The fight over Freedmen citizenship is often reduced to "membership policy," "rolls," or "sovereignty." But if we're honest, what we're really talking about is whether Cherokee Nationhood will be practiced through fear or through integrity through colonial categories or Cherokee values, through selective memory or full history.

The Cherokee Nation is not weak. Our sovereignty is not fragile. And our identity is not so brittle that it shatters when we tell the truth. What's fragile is a story that can't survive its own facts.

This conclusion pulls together the threads of this book and goes further: grounding the modern era in leadership, public education, and legal record; laying out a historical timeline; and naming the people inside the cases, because too many of them were turned into "et al." and forgotten like their lives didn't matter.

They did.

1) What This Book Proved

Cherokee citizenship existed before federal paperwork
Belonging was rooted in kinship, community responsibility, and lived relationships. Paper did not create Cherokee identity; it tried to manage and reshape it.

Slavery in Indian Country did not begin with Native nations
European colonists enslaved Indigenous people early, destabilized Native societies, and built the logic of commodifying human beings long before some Native nations were pressured into adopting chattel slavery.

"Freedman" is a federal legal label, later weaponized
It was a U.S. designation tied to emancipation, not a Cherokee cultural identity. In Native nations, it became an administrative category used to divide.

The 1866 Treaty promised citizenship to Freedmen and their descendants
Article 9 is clear: Freedmen and their descendants "shall have all the rights of native Cherokees."

Dawes-era categories manufactured separation
The Dawes Rolls were an allotment tool, not a sacred identity document. They froze earlier inconsistencies into inherited status.
Oklahoma's statehood and Jim Crow intensified racial sorting
Statehood added a surrounding regime of segregation that reinforced divisions already created by federal classification.

The modern battle is treaty logic vs. roll logic
Treaty logic says citizenship is binding.
Roll logic says a later federal category decides who counts.
Those are not equal frameworks.

2) Leadership That Chose the Truth

The Cherokee Nation's shift toward honesty and reconciliation did not happen in a vacuum. It happened because leaders at different moments, in different ways, chose truth over silence.

Deputy Principal Chief S. Joe Crittenden

Chief Crittenden was one of the earliest modern leaders to speak publicly and plainly about the need to honor Freedmen descendants' rights. His statements emphasized unity, responsibility, and the importance of facing the Nation's full history — not just the comfortable parts. He helped open the door for a more honest conversation inside the Cherokee Nation government.

Principal Chief Bill John Baker

After the 2017 federal decision confirming Freedmen descendants' right to citizenship, Chief Baker publicly welcomed Freedmen citizens and acknowledged that Freedmen ancestors walked the Trail of Tears with the Nation.

That mattered. It reframed the moment away from "outsiders pressing a claim" and back toward "our people carrying shared history.

Principal Chief Chuck Hoskin Jr.

Chief Hoskin has spoken even more directly about responsibility, equality, and reconciliation. In written testimony to Congress, he stated that the Cherokee Nation is "a better nation" for recognizing full and equal citizenship of Freedmen descendants, tying the obligation directly to Article 9 of the Treaty of 1866.

His public remarks connected to the Freedmen exhibit describe Freedmen citizens as "our Freedmen brothers and sisters" and emphasize commitment to reconciliation.

Leadership doesn't replace law or community, but leadership can change what a Nation believes it is allowed to say out loud.

That shift matters.

3) "We Are Cherokee" A Nation Putting Truth on the Wall

The "We Are Cherokee: Cherokee Freedmen and the Right to Citizenship" exhibit made a public statement that Cherokee Freedmen's history is part of the Cherokee Nation's story.

Its title says what this entire book has been saying:
We are Cherokee.
Not "we want to be."
Not "let us in."
Not "please approve us."
We are.

4) The Truth About Sovereignty

Sovereignty is not the right to forget.
It is the responsibility to govern with integrity.

A Nation that demands the United States honor treaties must honor its own treaty promises. Otherwise, "treaty" becomes a tool of convenience rather than a principle.

The deeper question has never been whether the Cherokee Nation has sovereignty.

The question is: What kind of sovereignty do we practice?

One rooted in Cherokee values, kinship, responsibility, truth, and honor.
Or one rooted in colonial categories, race boxes, roll logic, exclusion, and fear.
We Are Cherokee: A Nation Putting Truth on the Wall

5) A Historical Timeline of Cherokee Freedmen

A brief timeline showing cause and effect from slavery to treaty promise, to the roll-era division, to modern legal enforcement and public truth-telling.

1700s - 1830s: Colonial slavery expands

- Europeans enslave Indigenous people; captive markets destabilize Native nations.
- African chattel slavery grows into racial caste.

1830s: Removal
- Cherokee removal carries enslaved Black people west.
- Black families' Cherokee history becomes inseparable from the Nation's survival.

1861–1865: Civil War in Indian Territory
- Factional alignment and devastation.
- Enslaved people navigate war as danger and opportunity.

1866: Treaty of 1866
- Article 9 guarantees Freedmen and their descendants "all the rights of native Cherokees."

1898–1907: Dawes era
- Federal roll-making divides citizens into "by blood" vs. "Freedmen."
- Errors become permanent.

1907: Oklahoma statehood
- Jim Crow becomes law.
- Black Cherokee families face layered marginalization.

1975: Modern Cherokee Constitution
- Citizenship debates increasingly rely on roll categories.

2003–2008: Federal and tribal litigation intensifies
- Nero, Riggs, Allen, Vann, and others push the issue into the courts.

2017: Landmark federal decision
- Cherokee Nation v. Nash / Vann / Zinke enforces treaty-backed citizenship.

2020–present: Public truth-telling
- Equality initiatives expand.
- "We Are Cherokee" exhibit reframes from public memory.
preserved as in your draft, unchanged for accuracy and flow.

6) The People that History Tried to Turn into Paper

The system loves "rolls," "categories," and "et al." because those words erase people. But Cherokee Freedmen history is not a filing cabinet. It is families, churches, neighborhoods, and elders whose names kept getting turned into footnotes.

And I can't write this like it's distant because it isn't.

Bernice Riggs was not an abstract petitioner. She was an elder in my neighborhood and my Black Cherokee church.

Reverend Robert Nero wasn't just a caption. I fellowshipped with him at my church, at his church, and at other Black Cherokee churches across the Cherokee Nation.

Charlene White is not a line in a case. She is my cousin, and she was my next-door neighbor growing up. Her son was one of my closest family members.

Ralph Threat wasn't a legal reference. He's a U.S. veteran. And a family friend connected through some of my family, even though we are not directly kin. He is still always present at holidays, funerals, and celebrations.

These were not "issues."
They were people.

And when the record says "et al.," it's our job to say the names anyway.

Because the easiest way to erase a people is to keep their history but forget their faces.

7) Where the Cherokee Nation Is Now

Today, the Cherokee Nation recognizes Freedmen descendants as citizens and has taken concrete steps toward reconciliation through leadership, policy, public history, and institutional commitments to equality.

That does not mean every wound is healed.
It means the Nation has chosen a direction aligned with treaty obligation, public truth-telling, and Cherokee integrity.

And it means something else — something lived, not theoretical:

Recognizing Freedmen citizens did not destroy Cherokee identity.
It strengthened it.

The Nation is still Cherokee.
The language is still Cherokee.
Ceremonies are still Cherokee.
Families are still Cherokee.
And Tahlequah is still home.

Inclusion didn't dilute anything.
It exposed the lie that truth is dangerous.

I know this because I lived the opposite.

I grew up in the 1970s and 1980s, when the Cherokee Nation had very little money and very few services. Identity wasn't tied to benefits. It was tied to the community that raised you, who you knew, and where you showed up.

And in all that time, I never heard elders debate "Freedmen status."
They never used that term.

They only said we were Cherokee.

Some of us had cards. Some didn't.
But we were all Cherokees.
That distinction was about paperwork, not belonging.

And I moved through Native spaces, traditional Native communities, churches, powwows, and sports tournaments. I dated and married Native women, had kids, and started businesses all in Cherokee communities.
Not because I was claiming something.
But because it was already mine.
All my life, I have known I was a Black Cherokee.

Not as a contradiction.
Not as a qualifier.
Not as an argument.

It's simply who I am.

That lived reality is why the modern recognition of Freedmen descendant citizenship does not feel like a rupture. It feels like alignment, like the Nation catching up to what many of us already knew in our bones long before courts and councils said it out loud.
The truth didn't change Cherokee identity.
It finally told it straight.

Closing Statement
Being Cherokee is not about fear of dilution.
It is about honoring commitments, kinship, culture, history, and truth.
That truth includes the people who were enslaved.
It includes the people who were freed.
It includes intermarried and adopted people.
It includes the descendants who carried on Cherokee life.
It includes treaties.

It includes rolls and the damage they did.

It includes court fights.

It includes the museum walls where the Nation finally said it publicly:

We are Cherokee

Appendix A - Key Terms and Definitions

Cherokee Citizen

A person recognized as belonging to the Cherokee Nation under Cherokee law and treaty obligation. Historically grounded in kinship, community recognition, and responsibility, not race.

Black Cherokees

Cherokee citizens and community members of African descent whose families have lived within Cherokee society across generations before, during, and after removal, slavery, and statehood.

Freedman / Freedmen

A legal term used by the United States after the Civil War to describe formerly enslaved people. In Native nations, it became a federal administrative category. It was never a traditional Cherokee identity.

Cherokee Freedmen

Formerly enslaved people within the Cherokee Nation who were emancipated under the 1866 Treaty were recognized as citizens with full rights.

Cherokee Freedmen Descendants

Descendants of people emancipated under the 1866 Treaty who were promised citizenship and "all the rights of native Cherokees." Treaty citizenship extends to descendants.

Treaty of 1866 (*Cherokee Nation*)
A nation-to-nation agreement between the Cherokee Nation and the United States following the Civil War. Article 9 guarantees citizenship rights to Freedmen and their descendants.

Dawes Rolls
Federal enrollment lists were created to facilitate allotment (the breakup of communal tribal land). Not a cultural record of Cherokee identity. Contain documented errors, racial assumptions, and inconsistencies, and were built on earlier flawed rolls.

"By Blood"
A Dawes-era administrative category. Not a traditional Cherokee concept of belonging.

Blood Quantum
A federal invention used to measure Native identity in fractions. Designed for population control and reduction; not rooted in Cherokee tradition or science.

Fullblood (*Traditional Meaning*)
In Cherokee society, it meant living fully in Cherokee ways — language, culture, responsibility, not a mathematical fraction.

Fullblood (*Dawes Meaning*)
A numerical blood quantum assigned by Dawes workers, often estimated and not scientifically grounded.

Disenrollment
The removal of a person's citizenship status. For Freedmen descendants, disenrollment functioned as a modern form of removal from political belonging.

Appendix B - Major Treaties, Laws, and Policies Referenced

- Treaty of New Echota (1835) - Preceded removal; context for forced migration.

- Indian Removal Act (1830) - Enabled forced removal of Southeastern tribes.

- Treaty of 1866 (Cherokee Nation) - Guaranteed Freedmen citizenship.

- Dawes Act / Curtis Act Era (1898 - 1907) - Allotment and roll creation.

- Oklahoma Statehood (1907) - Imposed Jim Crow racial laws across Indian Territory.

- Cherokee Constitution (1975) - Modern governance framework.

- Federal Court Decision (2017) - Enforced the Treaty of 1866 citizenship rights.

Appendix C - Pre-Dawes Rolls and Record Issues

Before the Dawes Rolls, the Cherokee Nation and the United States produced multiple rolls for annuities, censuses, treaty compliance, and political administration. These records:

- used inconsistent naming and spelling
- reflected language barriers
- applied race unevenly
- often conflict with one another
- were never intended to permanently define identity

Some individuals listed as Freedmen on the Dawes Rolls were listed as "Cherokee by blood" on earlier rolls, demonstrating that Dawes categories were administrative choices, not definitive truth.

Appendix D - Condensed Historical Timeline

- 1700s–1800s: Enslavement of Native and African peoples under colonial systems
- 1830s: Cherokee removal west; Black Cherokees endure the Trail of Tears
- 1861–1865: Civil War in Indian Territory
- 1866: Treaty guarantees Freedmen citizenship
- 1898–1907: Dawes Rolls and allotment divide citizens on paper
- 1907: Oklahoma statehood; Jim Crow entrenched
- 1970s–1980s: Cherokee Nation survives with limited resources; identity lived through community
- 1989–2006: Early modern citizenship cases (Nero, Riggs, Allen)
- 2003–2017: Federal litigation culminating in treaty enforcement
- 2017–Present: Public recognition, reconciliation, and education initiatives

Appendix E - Key Citizenship Cases

(Reference List)

- Nero v. Cherokee Nation of Oklahoma (1989)
- Riggs v. Ummerteskee (2001)
- Allen v. Cherokee Nation Tribal Council (2004–2006)
- Vann v. Kempthorne (2003–2008)
- Cherokee Nation v. Nash, et al. (pre-2017)
- Cherokee Nation v. Nash, Vann, & Zinke (2017)
- In re Effect of Cherokee Nation v. Nash (implementation phase)
- Mayes v. Cherokee Nation Election Commission and Vann

(For full discussion of named parties and significance, see Conclusion.)

Appendix F - On Names, Memory, and "Et Al."

Legal records often replace people with shorthand et al.
This appendix affirms that history is carried by names, families, churches, neighborhoods, and relationships.

The individuals named in this book were not symbols.
They were citizens who bore the cost of truth-telling.

Remembering names is an act of restoration.

Appendix G - Author's Note on Lived Identity

The author grew up in Northeastern Oklahoma in the 1970s and 1980s, when the Cherokee Nation had few material resources and identity was not tied to benefits or paperwork. Community elders did not use the term Freedmen. They said:

We are Cherokee.

Participation in Native American communities, churches, sports tournaments, powwows, 49s, and intertribal community life shaped an understanding of belonging that predates modern policy debates.

This book is written from that lived ground.

Appendix H - Suggested Reading & Archival Sources

- Treaty texts and congressional records (U.S. National Archives)
- Cherokee Nation Supreme Court opinions
- Federal district and circuit court decisions
- Cherokee Nation public history projects and museum exhibits
- Oral histories from Cherokee and Black Cherokee communities

End of Appendix

AUTHOR'S NOTE

I wrote this book as a Cherokee historian and a Black Cherokee from Tahlequah. Not as an outsider studying Cherokee history, but as someone raised inside it. My earliest memories are Cherokee memories: church pews filled with familiar faces, basketball tournaments in all-Indian leagues, powwows where the drumbeat felt like home, and elders who never once questioned whether I belonged. They didn't use words like "Freedmen" or "by blood." They just said we were Cherokee.

This book grew out of that lived truth.

I didn't write it to win an argument. I wrote it because I've watched too many people I love, neighbors, cousins, elders, veterans, and church leaders get reduced to paperwork and "et al." in court cases. I wrote it because I've seen how colonial categories can be used to divide a Nation that survived removal, war, allotment, and statehood. I wrote it because the story of Black Cherokees is not a footnote. It is part of the spine.

I wrote it because the people who carried out this fight were not abstractions to me.

Bernice Riggs was an elder in my neighborhood and my Black Cherokee church. I mowed her grass.

Reverend Robert Nero was someone I fellowshipped with at my church, his church, and other Black Cherokee churches across the Cherokee Nation.

Charlene White is my cousin, and she was my next-door neighbor growing up. Her son was one of my closest family members.

Ralph Threat is a U.S. veteran and a family friend, connected through some of my people. Even though we aren't directly kin. I still see him at every Cherokee community event and family gatherings.

These are not case names. They are my people. I moved through Native spaces, traditional communities, churches, powwows, and sports tournaments. The way people move when they belong. Because I do belong. I dated and married Native women, raised Native children, and started businesses in Native American communities. Not because I was claiming something. But because it was already mine. I've always known I am Cherokee. Just like, I've always known I'm Black. It's who I am. It is who I've always been. It's who I will always be.

This book is my contribution to a truth that has always been bigger than paperwork: that Cherokee identity is lived, not assigned; that treaties matter; that kinship matters; that history matters; and that Black Cherokee families have been part of this Nation's story for centuries.

If this book does anything, I hope it helps us remember that telling the whole truth does not weaken the Cherokee Nation. It strengthens it. Because a Nation that knows its full story and honors all its people is a Nation that cannot be divided by paper. That is the Cherokee future I believe in.

Series Mission Statement

The Black Cherokee Series exists to restore the full, unbroken story of Black Cherokees, including free Black families who lived in Cherokee society before removal, Black people who married into Cherokee families and raised Cherokee descendants, and the Cherokee Freedmen and their descendants whose citizenship was guaranteed under the Treaty of 1866.

This series challenges colonial narratives, exposes the harm of roll-based identity, and centers the lived experiences of the people whose names were too often reduced to "et al." It honors the elders, ancestors, and descendants who carried Cherokee identity through silence, suspicion, and struggle.

The mission is simple:

To tell the truth.

To restore the record.

To honor the people.

To ensure Black Cherokee history is recognized as Cherokee history.

Summary

This book tells the story that has too often been pushed to the margins of Cherokee history: the story of Black Cherokees, Cherokee Freedmen, and their descendants who have lived, loved, built, worshiped, and survived inside the Cherokee Nation for centuries.

It traces the full arc of that history — from the colonial slave trade and the Trail of Tears, through the Civil War and the Treaty of 1866, through the Dawes Rolls and allotment, through Oklahoma statehood and Jim Crow, and into the modern legal battles that forced the Nation and the United States to confront the promises written in Article 9.

Across these chapters, one truth becomes clear:

Cherokee identity was never meant to be defined by federal paperwork.

It was lived through kinship, community, responsibility, and shared survival.

This book shows how colonial systems — rolls, blood quantum, racial categories, and disenrollment — attempted to divide a people who had already built a shared life. It exposes how the Dawes Rolls froze errors into law, how Jim Crow hardened racial boundaries, and how modern politics revived old divisions under a new language.

But it also documents the courage of those who refused to disappear:

the elders, neighbors, veterans, church leaders, and families who carried the truth forward even when the record tried to erase them. Their names, often reduced to "et al.," are restored here as part of the Nation's living memory.

The book follows the long legal struggle for recognition, culminating in the 2017 federal decision affirming that Freedmen descendants are citizens with "all the rights of native Cherokees," as promised in the Treaty of 1866. It highlights the leadership that chose truth, the institutions that began telling the full story, and the communities that never stopped living it.

At its core, this book is a declaration:

We are Cherokee.

Not because of a roll.

Not because of a fraction.

But because our families lived Cherokee history before removal, through removal, after removal, and into the present.

This is not a story of outsiders seeking entry.

It is a story of citizens reclaiming the truth that was always theirs. It is a call for a Cherokee future rooted not in fear, but in integrity. A future where the Nation honors its treaties, its history, and all its people.

SOCIAL MEDIA SUMMARY

Black Cherokee history is Cherokee history, and it's time to tell it whole.

Ty "GWY" Wilson, a Black Cherokee from Tahlequah, uncovers the full story: free Black families in Cherokee society, Black Cherokees who survived removal, the Freedmen promised citizenship in 1866, and the descendants who fought to keep that promise alive.

This book exposes the truth behind the Dawes Rolls, Jim Crow, modern citizenship battles, and restores the names and stories that history tried to erase.

If you care about Native history, Black history, or the fight for truth, this book belongs on your shelf.

Black Cherokees are Cherokee.

We always have been.

Press-Release Announcement

FOR IMMEDIATE RELEASE

New Multi-Volume Series Restores the Full History of Black Cherokees

Tahlequah, Oklahoma, author, historian, and filmmaker **Ty "GWY" Wilson**, a Black Cherokee from the Cherokee Nation of Oklahoma, announces the release of the Black Cherokee Series, a groundbreaking multi-book project documenting the complete, unbroken history of Black Cherokees.

The series covers the intertwined histories of:
- Black individuals who married into Cherokee families and their descendants
- Free Black people who lived in Cherokee society before removal and before U.S. jurisdiction
- Cherokee Freedmen and their descendants were guaranteed citizenship under the Treaty of 1866

Drawing from archival research, legal records, oral histories, and lived community experience, Wilson traces Black Cherokee history from the colonial Southeast through the Trail of Tears, the Civil War in Indian Territory, the Dawes Rolls, Oklahoma statehood, Jim Crow, and the modern legal battles that reaffirmed treaty-backed citizenship.

The series challenges long-standing misconceptions about Cherokee identity and exposes how federal policies attempted to divide people who had already built a shared life. It restores the names behind the court cases and honors the elders and families who preserved the truth across generations.

Wilson, who grew up in the Lee Street neighborhood of Tahlequah and participated in Native churches, powwows, sports tournaments, and community life, writes from lived experience rather than academic distance.

"This is Black Cherokee history. This is Cherokee history. This is our story told whole."

The first two books of the Black Cherokee Series are available now. There will be two more books released in 2026, with more to come. This series is available for educational institutions, libraries, tribal nations, cultural centers, and readers committed to truth, sovereignty, and historical restoration.

About the Author

Ty 'GWY' Wilson is a Cherokee Citizen, a Cherokee Historian, author, filmmaker, artist, and community advocate from Tahlequah, Oklahoma, the capital of the Cherokee Nation. Raised in the Lee Street neighborhood and shaped by the churches, families, and elders of Northeastern Oklahoma, Ty grew up inside Cherokee life not as an observer, but as a participant. His identity was formed long before paperwork or politics entered the conversation.

As a child of the 1970s and 1980s, Ty experienced the Cherokee Nation during a time when the Nation had few material resources and identity lived through community rather than benefits. He moved through traditional Native spaces, communities, churches, powwows, 49s, sports tournaments, and intertribal family gatherings. The way people move when they belong. He dated and married Native women, raised Native children, and built businesses in Cherokee communities. Not because he was claiming something, but because it was already his.

Ty's work is grounded in the lived truth that Black Cherokee families have always been part of Cherokee history in Oklahoma. His writing centers the stories of elders, neighbors, and kin whose names were too often reduced to "et al." in court cases or erased in public narratives. People like Bernice Riggs, an elder from his neighborhood and church; Reverend Robert Nero, a spiritual leader he fellowshipped with across Black Cherokee churches; Charlene White, his cousin and next-door neighbor growing up; and Ralph Threat, a U.S. veteran and family friend connected through shared community ties. Their lives, not just their case names, form the backbone of his work.

Ty is a co-founder of the CBIHP Foundation and serves on the boards of the Oklahoma Blues Hall of Fame, the Bare Bones Film Festival, and the Cherokee Nation Freedmen History Advisory Committee. His creative work spans multiple media, including documentary films, music, visual art, and public history projects. He has collaborated with cultural institutions, museums, universities, and community organizations across the United States to preserve and uplift Black Cherokee and Native American histories.

His book series, including Black Cherokees, and 1st American, and Oklahoma Black Cherokees, reflects decades of research, community engagement, and personal experience. Through writing, filmmaking, and public speaking, Ty works to ensure that the full truth of Cherokee history is told: the truth that includes the enslaved, the freed, the adopted, the intermarried, and the descendants who carried Cherokee life forward.

Ty's mission is simple and unwavering:

To honor the ancestors, restore the record, and tell the truth without fear.

He writes from lived ground, from community memory, and from a lifelong understanding that identity is not granted by paperwork; it is lived, inherited, and carried.

BACK COVER PHOTO

A photo of **Jessie Mae (Cooper) Coulter**'s funeral rug.

by Ty 'GWY' Wilson

Find more Cherokee books by CBIHP members at

www.**cbihpfoundation.org/cbihp-books.html**

You can also **scan the QR code** below.

SHORT SUMMARY

A groundbreaking historical work that restores the full, unbroken story of Black Cherokees, including free Black families who lived in Cherokee society before removal, Black people who married into Cherokee families and raised Cherokee descendants, and the Cherokee Freedmen and their descendants, promised citizenship under the Treaty of 1866.

Written by Ty "GWY" Wilson, a Cherokee historian and a Black Cherokee from Tahlequah, this book traces Cherokee history from the colonial Southeast through the Trail of Tears, the Civil War in Indian Territory, the Dawes Rolls and allotment, Oklahoma statehood and Jim Crow, and into the modern legal battles that reaffirmed treaty-backed citizenship. Combining lived experience, community memory, legal analysis, and historical research, this volume challenges colonial narratives and centers the people whose names were too often reduced to "et al."

A vital contribution to Cherokee history, Native studies, African American history, and the ongoing national conversation about identity, sovereignty, and truth.